Creating Dialogue for TV

As entertaining as it is enlightening, *Creating Dialogue for TV: Screenwriters Talk Television* presents interviews with five Hollywood professionals who talk about all things related to dialogue – from naturalistic style to the building of characters to swearing and dialect.

Screenwriters/showrunners David Mandel (*Curb Your Enthusiasm, Veep*), Jane Espenson (*Buffy, Battlestar Galactica, Once Upon a Time*), Robert Berens (*Supernatural*), Sheila Lawrence (*Gilmore Girls, Ugly Betty, The Marvelous Mrs. Maisel*), and Doris Egan (*Tru Calling, House, Reign*) field a linguist's inquiries about the craft of writing dialogue. This book is for anyone who has ever wondered what creative processes and attitudes lie behind the words they encounter when tuning into their favorite television show. It provides direct insights into Hollywood writers' knowledge and opinions of how language is used in television narratives, and in doing so shows how language awareness, attitudes, and the craft of using words are utilized to create popular TV series. The book will appeal to students and teachers in screenwriting, creative writing, and linguistics as well as lay readers.

Monika Bednarek is Associate Professor in the Department of Linguistics at the University of Sydney, Australia. She has authored six academic books, most recently *Language and Television Series: A Linguistic Approach to TV Dialogue* (2018). Her research interests include corpus linguistics, discourse analysis, media linguistics, sociolinguistics, and the linguistic expression of emotion and attitude.

Routledge Studies in Media Theory & Practice

1 **Semiotics and Title Sequences**
Text-Image Composites in Motion Graphics
Authored by Michael Betancourt

2 **Synchronization and Title Sequences**
Audio-Visual Semiosis in Motion Graphics
Authored by Michael Betancourt

3 **Title Sequences as Paratexts**
Narrative Anticipation and Recapitulation
Authored by Michael Betancourt

4 **The Screenwriters Taxonomy**
A Collaborative Approach to Creative Storytelling
Authored by Eric R. Williams

5 **Open Space New Media Documentary**
A Toolkit for Theory and Practice
Patricia R. Zimmermann and Helen De Michiel

6 **Film & TV Tax Incentives in the U.S.**
Courting Hollywood
Authored by Glenda Cantrell and Daniel Wheatcroft

7 **Typography and Motion Graphics: The 'Reading-Image'**
Authored by Michael Betancourt

Creating Dialogue for TV

Screenwriters Talk Television

Monika Bednarek

THE UNIVERSITY OF SYDNEY

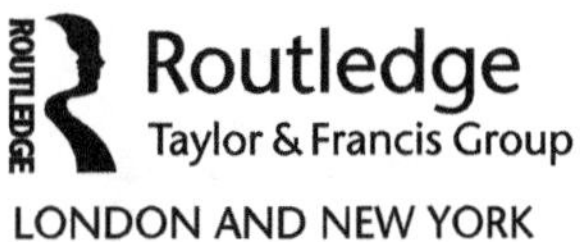

LONDON AND NEW YORK

First published 2019 by Routledge

2 Park Square, Milton Park, Abingdon, Oxon OX14 4RN
605 Third Avenue, New York, NY 10017

Routledge is an imprint of the Taylor & Francis Group, an informa business

First issued in paperback 2021

British Library Cataloguing-in-Publication Data
A catalogue record for this book is available from the British Library

Library of Congress Cataloging-in-Publication Data
Names: Bednarek, Monika, 1977– author.
Title: Creating dialogue for TV : screenwriters talk television / Monika Bednarek.
Description: London ; New York : Routledge, 2019. | Series: Routledge studies in media theory & practice ; 8 | Includes bibliographical references.
Identifiers: LCCN 2018051584 | ISBN 9780367139582 (hardback: alk. paper) | ISBN 9780429029394 (e-book : alk. paper)
Subjects: LCSH: Television authorship. | Dialogue. | Television writers—Interviews.
Classification: LCC PN1992.7 .B34 2019 | DDC 808.2/25—dc23
LC record available at https://lccn.loc.gov/2018051584

ISBN: 978-0-367-13958-2 (hbk)
ISBN: 978-1-03-217840-0 (pbk)
DOI: 10.4324/9780429029394

Typeset in Times New Roman
by Apex CoVantage, LLC

Contents

Images

Acknowledgments

The interviews for this book were undertaken during my sabbatical in the first half of 2017 at the University of California, Santa Barbara (UCSB). I would like to thank the Department of Linguistics at UCSB for hosting my visit and Professor Mary Bucholtz for being my Faculty sponsor. The University of Sydney provided institutional and financial support, for which I am very grateful. I also want to thank Georgia Carr, who expertly transcribed all interviews.

I am extremely thankful to the five Hollywood screenwriters/showrunners whom I interviewed for this book: Jane Espenson, David Mandel, Doris Egan, Bob Berens, and Sheila Lawrence. Special thanks are due to Jane Espenson, who was extremely generous with her time and assistance. I also appreciate the help from Javier Barrios and Hilary Swett regarding access to official final scripts archived in the Writers Guild Foundation's Shavelson-Webb Library in Los Angeles. I am grateful to Sheni Kruger, Sarah Pickles, and the Routledge production team for seeing the manuscript through to publication. I would also like to thank the anonymous reviewer who provided feedback on earlier draft chapters of the manuscript. Last, but not least, I am grateful to the five screenwriters and the Television Academy for permission to use the photos to accompany the biographical notes in this book.

1 Introduction

If cinema is said to be a director's medium, then in the world of television it is the writers who rule.[1] There is no doubt that many industry professionals play an important role in creating the TV series that so captivate our attention – from directors to actors to cinematographers, and so on. Yet, it all starts with the writing team. In the famous writers' room,[2] television screenwriters jointly come up with the stories that we encounter when we tune into our favorite shows. But with the exception of a few well-known showrunners, viewers often don't know who these writers are or how they work.

In this book, I present extracts from my interviews with five Hollywood screenwriters: David Mandel (*Curb Your Enthusiasm*, *Veep*), Jane Espenson (*Buffy, Battlestar Galactica, Once Upon a Time*), Sheila Lawrence (*Gilmore Girls, Ugly Betty, The Marvelous Mrs. Maisel*), Robert Berens (*Supernatural*), and Doris Egan (*Tru Calling, House, Reign*). Although some are showrunners, I use the shorthand "writers" or "screenwriters" to refer to them in this book. As a linguist, I am particularly interested in what they have to say about language use in TV narratives. After all, it is through language – using words in utterances – that characters are created and that stories are told. In this book you will find out what these writers say about what makes great dialogue, how to build a character through language, and how to express emotion through dialogue. You will also learn about their views on swearing and on particular expressions like *ain't* or *y'all*. They will tell you what they think are the main differences between how TV characters use language and how people speak in the "real" world. The interviews also include many interesting anecdotes and observations about the series that the writers have worked on.

This book is therefore aimed at anyone interested in the craft of screenwriting, including students and teachers in screenwriting or creative writing as well as lay readers. It is for any reader wanting to find out more about language use in TV series and about writing the dialogue sections in a TV script. The book *directly* presents the words of the five industry professionals, rather than providing a critical scholarly analysis or comprehensive synthesis of what they say. In this sense, the book also offers primary material that others can use in their own research, including scholars in screenwriting studies, film, television and media production, and linguistics.

Of course, there is a wealth of existing material available on writing dialogue for television series. There are scholarly works by academics investigating screenwriting; there are handbooks or manuals on how to write for television; and there are interviews with TV writers or showrunners (some of which can be found online). However, apart from a few exceptions this material does not focus specifically on language.[3] It is this unique focus on language and dialogue that makes this book a distinctive and special contribution to television writing. We live in an era that has been called a new golden age of television. TV shows are being praised and awarded for their writing (for example through the Emmy award categories) – thus, I strongly believe it is high time we paid more attention to their language use.

Although I am based in the Department of Linguistics at the University of Sydney, I interviewed the five industry professionals while I was on research leave at the University of California, Santa Barbara. Three writers were interviewed face-to-face while I was in Los Angeles, while two were interviewed via Skype from Santa Barbara (Goleta). Because the interviews differed in length, not all screenwriters answered all questions. In this book I only present the answers to the questions that I asked all five industry professionals.[4] I have edited their answers somewhat for readability, although I have tried to preserve the "spoken" flavor. Keenly aware of the busy nature of an industry professional's life, I am extremely grateful for their cooperation. I would of course have liked to have interviewed additional writers with different backgrounds, and would be very happy to include such in a potential second edition of this book.[5]

It is worth noting that these interviews are part of a larger research project that was written up in the scholarly monograph *Language and Television Series: A Linguistic Approach to TV Dialogue* (Cambridge University Press, 2018). In this project I explored TV series from three perspectives, including production (creation), product (dialogue), and consumption (viewers). The interviews with screenwriters that I present in this book are part of the project component that focused on the *creation* of dialogue. As working industry professionals, writers have very specific views and attitudes about language and it is therefore interesting to look at what they say about how they create dialogue for TV series. Some of the observations from these interviews have been incorporated in my research monograph, which includes several citations from the five screenwriters. Here I offer their fuller responses to a number of the key questions concerning TV dialogue.[6] In addition, the book you are reading now consists of edited and curated interview material rather than being a critical academic monograph. As such, its main audience are students, screenwriting teachers, budding screenwriters, and lay readers – who can all use this book to hear from industry professionals who present their own perspectives and experiences about creating dialogue for TV. The book is an attempt to share some of my interview data so that it may be useful for others. By focusing specifically on language use, this book can complement existing resources in this field: as part of the larger research project that I mentioned above, I examined 14 manuals on how to write for television to find out to what extent such material discusses language. I discovered that explicit or in-depth description of how to use language is rare, and that the manuals focus much more on structural or narrative aspects.

This book is structured into a series of short chapters covering interview questions and responses about a specific topic: in *On great dialogue*, each interviewee discusses how "great" (high-quality) dialogue could be defined. In the next chapter (*On naturalism*), writers explain differences between how characters speak in TV series and how people speak in "real" life. For example, just how naturalistic should TV dialogue be? They also give their opinions on specific words and phrases like *you know, well*, and *like*. This is followed by a chapter dedicated to the expression of emotion. How do writers tell us that a character is feeling a particular emotion? How can dialogue, as opposed to the actors' performance, play a role? This chapter focuses on interviewees' answers to such questions. The focus on character continues in the chapter *On building characters through language*. Whether we love or hate them, TV characters are their own personalities. In this chapter, interviewees tell us how writers build characters through language and how language differentiates characters from each other. In the next chapter, *On swearing*, I present industry professionals' views on the use of swearing/cursing, which often attracts censorship. The final chapter before the conclusion, *On dialect*, presents writers' views on how to represent dialects in TV series, especially when they themselves are not part of the relevant community of speakers. The chapter explicitly addresses stigmatized or stereotypical expressions like *ain't* and *y'all* but also includes more general discussion.

Each of the chapters concludes with a summary that also presents readers with brief advice, mainly based on the screenwriters' answers but occasionally supplemented by insights from my own research. Despite the inclusion of these advice sections, the book is first and foremost intended as a collection of interviews rather than a "how to" manual. In addition, the brief summaries do not attempt to link the interview answers to the wider body of research on television dialogue that exists in linguistics and other disciplines or to compare it to existing advice in screenwriting manuals. Such critical scholarly treatment can be found in the aforementioned research monograph *Language and Television Series*. The concluding chapter addresses five important points in relation to the advice sections, such as differences between scripts and on-screen dialogue, and issues to do with authorship.

Together, the interview material collected in this book provides fascinating insights into the language awareness, attitudes, and craft of using words to create popular TV series that are consumed by millions of viewers around the world.

Notes

1 David Lavery and Cynthia Burkhead, eds., *Joss Whedon: Conversations* (Jackson, MS: University Press of Mississippi, 2011), vii.
2 Tim Adams, "Secrets of the TV writers' room: Inside *Narcos*, *Transparent* and *Silicon Valley*," *The Guardian/The Observer*, September 24, 2017.
3 A review of this existing material, with relevant references, is provided in Monika Bednarek, *Language and Television Series: A Linguistic Approach to TV Dialogue* (Cambridge: Cambridge University Press, 2018). A bibliography of linguistic research on TV series can be found in Monika Bednarek and Raffaele Zago, "Bibliography of linguistic research on fictional (narrative, scripted) television series and films/movies," *Version 2*, February 2018. A very recent addition to interview-based books on screenwriting is Patricia Phalen's *Writing Hollywood* (London/New York: Routledge, 2018), which focuses on television.
4 One answer was not included at the request of the interviewee. The writers were interviewed between March and May 2017. I initially used Twitter to contact Jane Espenson, who has a background herself in linguistics. During our interview, she kindly offered to put me in touch with other screenwriters who might also be willing to be interviewed. At that point, I was especially interested in interviewing writers who had created dialogue for one of the series that I was covering in an academic book (*Language and Television Series*). That's why I asked Jane to identify writers for these particular series. I then contacted the suggested writers and interviewed those who responded to my email and agreed to be interviewed. The face-to-face interviews took place at a hotel restaurant, at a writer's office, and at a writer's home. Each interview lasted between half an hour and two hours depending on the availability of the interviewees. I used a method called "semi-structured interview", which allows a more conversation-like interview where the interviewer asks follow-up questions or goes with the flow of the discussion. In editing the answers for this book, I have mainly taken out repetitions, deleted some words and phrases (like *you know, I mean, like*), and sometimes tidied up the structure a little, improved the flow, or introduced clarifications. The screenwriters were also given the opportunity to check their transcripts and suggest minor stylistic changes that did not compromise the integrity of the original interview. All in all, the spoken nature of the interviews is still very much apparent.
5 My contact information can be found on my university website: http://sydney.edu.au/arts/linguistics/staff/profiles/monika.bednarek.php
6 The questions that I asked in the interviews are included in the relevant chapters that follow. Sometimes the question was not posed because a relevant answer

had already been given in relation to a previous question. In some interviews, follow-up questions were used to elicit further details. I don't provide these in the manuscript; neither do I provide all variants of the questions asked.

References

Adams, Tim. "Secrets of the TV writers' room: Inside *Narcos*, *Transparent* and *Silicon Valley*." *The Guardian/The Observer*, September 24, 2017. www.theguardian.com/tv-and-radio/2017/sep/23/secrets-of-the-tv-writers-rooms-tv-narcos-silicon-valley-transparent.

Bednarek, Monika. *Language and Television Series: A Linguistic Approach to TV Dialogue*. Cambridge: Cambridge University Press, 2018.

Bednarek, Monika and Raffaele Zago. "Bibliography of linguistic research on fictional (narrative, scripted) television series and films/movies." *Version 2*, February 2018. www.academia.edu/30703199/Bednarek_M._and_Zago_R._2018._Bibliography_of_linguistic_research_on_fictional_narrative_scripted_television_series_and_films_movies_version_2_February_2018_.

Lavery, David and Cynthia Burkhead, eds., *Joss Whedon: Conversations*. Jackson, MS: University Press of Mississippi, 2011.

Phalen, Patricia F. *Writing Hollywood: The Work and Professional Culture of Television Writers*. London/New York: Routledge, 2018.

2 The writers/showrunners

David Mandel

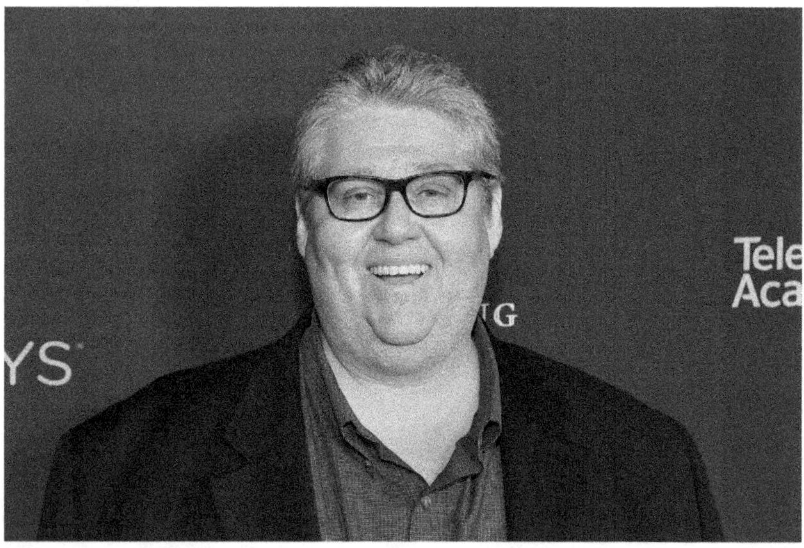

Image 2.1 David Mandel

Source: Photograph © Television Academy, used with permission

David Mandel is the two-time Emmy Award-winning showrunner and Executive Producer of *Veep*. He also wrote for such shows as *Saturday Night Live* (92–95), *Seinfeld*, where he wrote "The Bizarro Jerry" (aka "Man-Hands") and "The Betrayal" (the "backwards" episode with Peter Mehlman), *Curb Your Enthusiasm*, and even an episode of *The Simpsons* ("Treehouse of Horror XXIII" with Brian Kelley). He is the co-writer of *Eurotrip* and *The Dictator* and, if you press him on it, *The Cat in the Hat*. His directing credits include *Veep* (Emmy Award-nominated for "Kissing Your Sister"), *Curb Your Enthusiasm, The Comedians,* and *Eurotrip* (uncredited). He is the co-author of "Star Wars Art: Ralph McQuarrie", and an avid collector of original comic book art and Star Wars memorabilia – and movie props if you have any to sell.

Selected credits: *Veep, Curb Your Enthusiasm, Seinfeld*

Doris Egan

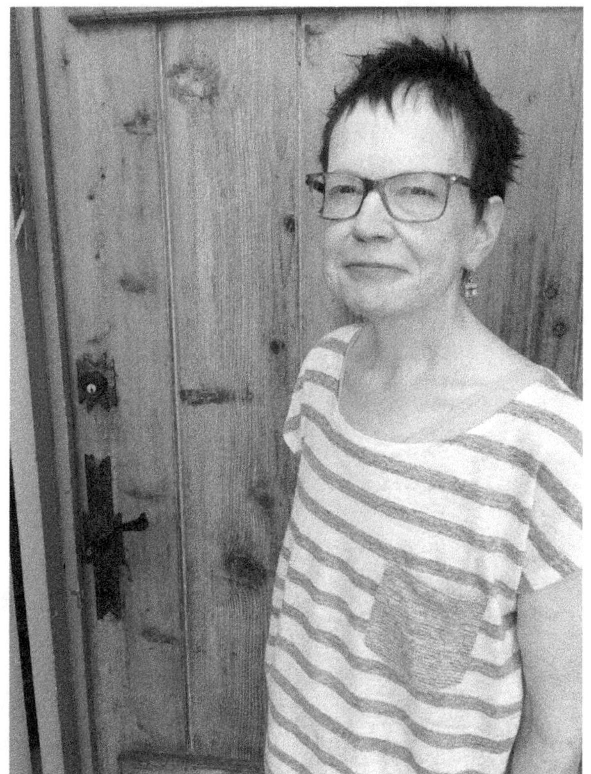

Image 2.2 Doris Egan

Source: Photograph supplied by Doris Egan, used with permission

Doris Egan is an Emmy Award-nominated writer and producer who has worked on television dramas such as *Reign*, *Torchwood*, *House*, *Smallville*, *Early Edition*, and *The Agency*. Doris is also a novelist and short story writer who is known for her sci-fi/fantasy *Gate of Ivory* trilogy. She lives in a house in the hills with a garden, two dogs, and too many books, where she misses red and gold autumns and the time to write novels.

Selected credits: *Reign, House, Tru Calling, The Agency, Smallville, Dark Angel*

Sheila Lawrence

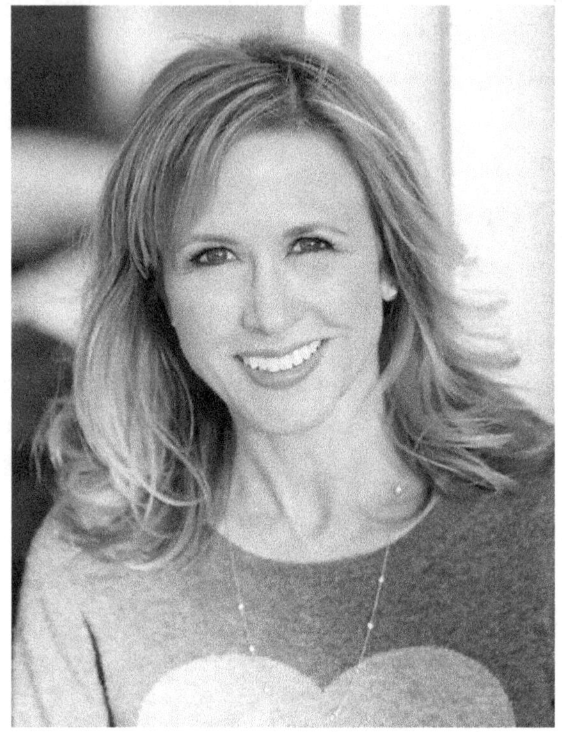

Image 2.3 Sheila Lawrence

Source: Photograph by Joy Peters Photography, used with permission

Sheila Lawrence has written both comedy and drama, but she most enjoys being at the intersection of the two genres. To that end, she executive produced the award-winning *Ugly Betty* (Golden Globe, WGA award, Emmy nomination) while under an overall deal at ABC Studios. Her long list of credits also includes *Gilmore Girls*, *Desperate Housewives*, *Imposters*, and Amazon's critically acclaimed *The Marvelous Mrs. Maisel* (Golden Globe, Emmy, Critics' Choice, Producers' Guild Award). She is married to fellow television writer, Breen Frazier, and has two sons . . . who she hopes will one day enter a sensible profession.

Selected credits: *Ugly Betty, The Marvelous Mrs. Maisel, Gilmore Girls, Hart of Dixie, Desperate Housewives, Mad About You*

Robert Berens

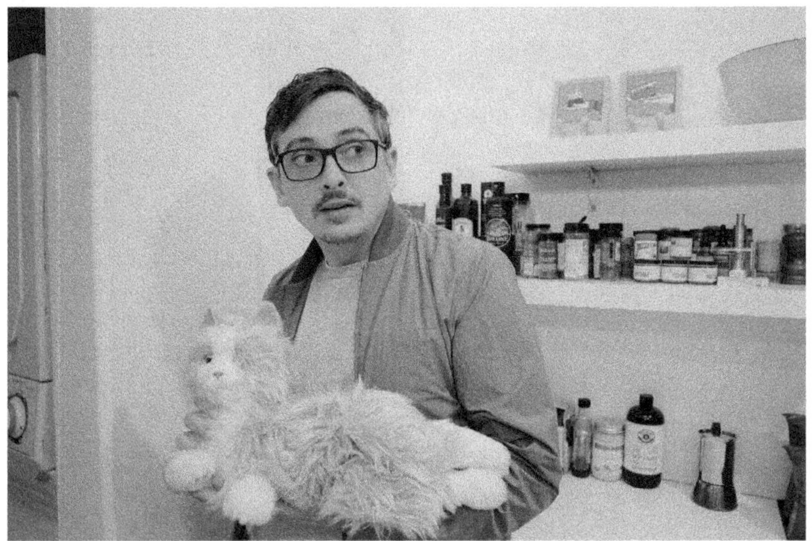

Image 2.4 Robert Berens

Source: Photograph by Spencer Moore, used with permission

Robert Berens (sometimes known as "Bob" or "Bobo") is a Los Angeles based writer and producer. He has written for the shows *Ringer* and *Supernatural*. He also loves cats.

Selected credits: *Supernatural, Ringer*

Jane Espenson

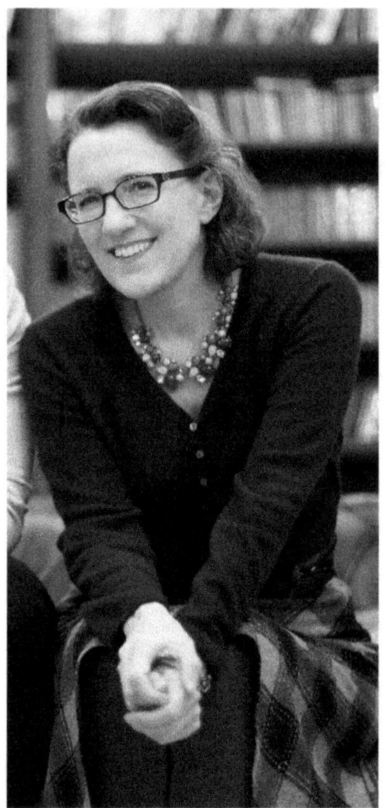

Image 2.5 Jane Espenson

Source: Photo credit: Matt Sayles, used with permission

Jane Espenson is a writer/producer best known for her work on *Buffy the Vampire Slayer, Firefly, Battlestar Galactica, Once Upon a Time*, and other series, often in the sci-fi and fantasy genres. She has the singular distinction of having written material for the *Star Trek*, *Star Wars*, Whedonverse, *Dr. Who*, Marvel, DC, and Battlestar universes. She also writes comic books, short stories, and essays. Jane lives in Los Angeles and loves cheese, dogs, and cheese dogs.

Selected credits: *Once Upon a Time, Battlestar Galactica, Buffy the Vampire Slayer*

3 On great dialogue

Introductory remarks

Television writer Larry Brody suggests that there is "a generally accepted definition" for good dialogue, as being "concise, witty, believable, and revealing of human character and emotion".[1] But is there such a consensus among screenwriters? And how easy is it really to define good television dialogue? To find out, I asked each of the five writers a question such as "how would you define great dialogue in TV series?"

David Mandel

It's hard to explain [how to define great dialogue]. I'd love to tell you that I always know it on the page, but I do believe it's about the ear, it's about hearing it. There are things that seem good and then they are performed and they're not, and vice versa. I'm always telling new writers "read your own scripts out loud before they ever get to actors". And I still stand by that, because you can write something, but it's not until you read it yourself that the faults just show themselves. If you can't read it clearly, if you stumble, *they*'re going to stumble, there's something off. And so for me, it's all about smoothness to the ear. That's great dialogue. I lean towards what people might call snappy, peppy dialogue, that's the kind of dialogue I like. But even serious or very serious dialogue, there's a smoothness that the ear recognizes that I would call great dialogue.

Doris Egan

I don't know that it [great dialogue] is definable. There was a famous definition in the US by a judge who was trying to define pornography, because pornography has so often been illegal, but what is it? And he said, "I don't know what it is, but I can point to it". And to a great extent that's dialogue.

I was on a panel at the Writers' Guild a few months ago and we were talking about dialogue. And the other panelists were talking about how every character should have their own unique voice. And I can't argue with that, and they talked about making dialogue very realistic – and I'm not going to argue with that either. However, I will often enjoy listening to dialogue that is full of artifice and is not realistic in the slightest. And to state the obvious, I don't think Shakespearian monologue is at all realistic to anyone. The example that I gave at the time was Aaron Sorkin [*The West Wing*]. His characters to me all sound alike, and I'm okay with that. I'm not watching one of his shows because I want a gritty cross-section of American life. I'm looking for a little entertainment and quite often he can deliver. The comparison I'm going to make might sound wrong, but well-done dialogue is like audible poetry. They're not going to say something too long or too short, it's going to have the right rising, the right falling – I could compare it to music but I don't want to imply it's musical and lilting, I don't necessarily mean that. But it is sort of like pornography: you can point to it.

Sheila Lawrence

I think great dialogue captures the reality of the way people speak, but then elevates it a little bit, with language that is perhaps even a tad more eloquent than you would use in "real" life, if that makes sense. That's probably the most ideal situation, but I also think the realism of the dialogue is the most important. When I'm writing [dialogue], I hear it in my head – almost, I would imagine, as composers hear music. You hear the rhythm, you hear if it jumps off the page at you, if it sounds false, if it sounds stilted or not the way people would actually speak.

Robert Berens

I don't think I have a hard and fast answer to that. But it's something I think about when so much is dependent on context and you sometimes, in the pursuit, say, of novelty you try having a character say something they haven't already said multiple times. But sometimes the best dialogue is the simplest. Or if it's happening in the right place in the story, even if it's something that the character has already said before, sometimes that's the right thing to say. And sometimes the dialogue that's the best is the most elaborate and you're looking for the freshest, newest expression that they can make. So really it's a matter of context and author and showrunner judgment about when it's good to be simple and when it's okay to be complex. And of course, there's always the issue of in-character – would this character say this? So that becomes a kind of boundary on how characters will speak or how they'll express themselves. And I think that it's always an open conversation and it's never fully resolved. Even with our characters [in *Supernatural*], I think that different writers have different approaches about how articulate they are. And sometimes you might move towards making them sound almost academic in their expressions and it's sophisticated, complex language. And then other writers will push back and they feel that Sam and Dean [*Supernatural* characters] – particularly Dean – consist of more of a blue-collar diction and lexicon. And also there's flexibility and it goes back and forth and Dean – if you look at the history of the show – sometimes makes fairly astute, intellectual, piercing, penetrating, articulate points, and sometimes he gets played for a sort of cave man, for laughs. And I think it's always in flux.

One show that I've adored in the past year or two is *Rectify*. It's excellent. And that's a case where the dialogue has a kind of elevated quality, but it also is very simple. And there's just a purity and simplicity to that show and the way that show is wrought. But it's also a realist show. It's not a genre show and it isn't subordinate to the machinery, the mechanics of plot, in the way that a network genre necessarily is.

Jane Espenson

I think the number one mistake that many writers of dialogue make is to write from what they've heard on other TV shows, and even very experienced writers will do it. So if a character walks into a room and another character says "to what do I owe this honor?" or "I don't believe I've had the privilege" – all those phrases that people on TV say all the time, but that nobody's really said in spontaneous American dialogue in 40 years – those are when you can tell the writers are thinking too much about what this sounds like as a show, instead of what it sounds like as people. So I'm always trying to write things only people say, leave in mistakes, leave in ungrammaticalities – anything that makes that character seem really breathing and human.

Now, other writers would disagree about this. There are definitely writers who would look at dialogue I write and say it's loose and too unfocused – you could do this in fewer syllables, this bit's extraneous. And their point is well taken. Generally, a tight script is a good thing, there's no fat on it. "Tight" means economical, the fewest syllables. But I think verisimilitude is important – sound like people. There's an example Ron Moore talked about in one of the commentaries he did on an episode of *Battlestar Galactica*. It was before I was there, but it was a moment that struck me when I watched it and then I got to hear him talk about it. There's a bit where the president and the admiral are on the phone with each other and there's some horrible crisis they have to decide and they both fall silent. And after a beat of silence, one of them says "are you still there?" – "Oh, yeah, yeah, I'm still here, I'm just thinking". Ron said "you cut story, but you keep character moments like that, because that moment of two people on the phone is what makes you feel like 'oh that could be me, I've said that a million times – Wait did I lose you?'" It's not economical, but it's exactly the kind of dialogue that's worth keeping.

So dialogue should be realistic. This includes things like characters misunderstanding or mishearing each other – which almost nobody writes, because you don't have the room. TV writing has to be so tight, because you get 42 minutes. And, increasingly, you don't even get to write long scenes during those 42 minutes because you have less time between commercial breaks. TV shows used to be four acts, four bits between commercials. Now there's six. So you have less time between each commercial break and I think this has the effect of making it a necessity to keep the show even more always "on story". So it's a real luxury these days; you never get a long scene. I've been on shows in the past where we would not infrequently have a six-page scene. It'd be very rare to see that now on a network show. Cable or streaming – that can be a whole other thing. *The Crown* [Netflix] can do a six-page scene. But on network you have to keep things trotting along, because you're heading for that act break. So it's a real luxury to get to do a moment that's just pure character. The moment on the phone of the admiral and the president is more than just "oh I've done that myself". It's also "oh those are two people who talk on the phone the way really good friends do, where they're willing to let a silence happen, because they know the other person will need to think about it". And it tells you a lot about characters. So the best bits of dialogue are those where it is real and human and a thing you don't normally see on TV, *and* it tells you something about these characters in this moment. It's not something everyone can do; it's not something everyone values; it's not something that some shows are about. But I feel that a moment like that, it helps the script really sing.

Summary and advice

The responses here suggest that it is not easy to define "great dialogue" and that there are no criteria that everyone would agree on. Often, the writers define it as something they cannot explicitly define, but can recognize (or hear) when they encounter it. Some of the relevant dimensions mentioned by the writers in these interviews include smoothness or rhythm, realism, and characterization, but they also mention that there is a lot of variation depending on the type of TV series we are talking about.

While these five writers do not mention it here, another writer, Pamela Douglas, advises that dialogue should be multifunctional: no scene should merely explore character or be used only for exposition.[2] My own research has revealed that much TV dialogue is indeed multifunctional.[3] One piece of general advice for creating good dialogue is thus to keep in mind the many different purposes or functions for which dialogue in TV series is used. When writing, ask yourself "what is the purpose of this piece of dialogue?" For example, dialogue can function to establish the setting – where and when a scene takes place. Dialogue can also function to move the story forward. Dialogue can provide crucial information about past or future happenings. Dialogue establishes who the characters are and their relationships to other characters. Dialogue can tell audiences that this character is a "villain" who should not be trusted. Dialogue can be used to tell a joke or otherwise entertain the audience or to create emotional responses in viewers. Dialogue can function to create realism or to establish consistency and continuity across episodes. Dialogue can sometimes work to convey a moral message. When writing a piece of dialogue, think about all the different functions that dialogue can fulfill and try to make each line of dialogue fulfill more than one function. Have a look at the following example from the pilot episode of *The Big C* (Showtime, 2010–2013):

CATHY: We didn't have a lot of money growing up but we did have a pool in our backyard. My brother and I, we would spend all summer in it making up dives. My signature was the banana split and dive.

DOCTOR: Sounds fun.

CATHY: Except when Sean would hold me under the water and fart on my face.

This piece of dialogue clearly fulfills multiple functions at once: the protagonist (Cathy) discloses information about her childhood, which provides a motivation for why she wants to install a pool in her backyard (as seen at the beginning of this episode). This is also the first mention of Sean and introduces this character to viewers explicitly as Cathy's brother (*My brother and I . . . Sean*). The dialogue also tells us more about the character's biography (not being rich, her childhood experiences) and her relationship to her brother as a child. Finally, the last line creates humor. So this is a good example of multifunctional dialogue.[4]

Notes

1 Cited in Kay Richardson, *Television Dramatic Dialogue: A Sociolinguistic Study* (Oxford: Oxford University Press, 2010), 75.

2 Pamela Douglas, *Writing the TV Drama Series: How to Succeed as a Professional Writer in TV* (Studio City, CA: Michael Wiese Productions, 2011), 112, 114.
3 Monika Bednarek, *Language and Television Series: A Linguistic Approach to TV Dialogue* (Cambridge: Cambridge University Press, 2018).
4 Additional information about the different functions of TV dialogue and further examples from TV series can be found at www.syd-tv.com and in Chapters 3–4 of: Monika Bednarek, *Language and Television Series: A Linguistic Approach to TV Dialogue* (Cambridge: Cambridge University Press, 2018).

References

Bednarek, Monika. *Language and Television Series: A Linguistic Approach to TV Dialogue*. Cambridge: Cambridge University Press, 2018.

Douglas, Pamela. *Writing the TV Drama Series: How to Succeed as a Professional Writer in TV*, 3rd edition. Studio City, CA: Michael Wiese Productions, 2011.

Richardson, Kay. *Television Dramatic Dialogue: A Sociolinguistic Study*. Oxford: Oxford University Press, 2010.

4 On naturalism

Introductory remarks

One of the key concerns of scholars interested in examining how language is used in television series has been naturalism. For example, linguist Douglas Biber poses the following questions:

> Don't we talk just like people on television? Or rather, don't those people talk just like us? Conversations on television seem completely natural to the normal viewer. But is that because we have come to expect a particular style of interaction on TV, or because those interactions accurately capture the actual linguistic characteristics of everyday conversation?[1]

Many linguists try to answer these questions by comparing dialogue from TV series with unscripted conversation. A less common approach is to examine manuals and writers' blogs for insights from screenwriters.[2] In my interviews with the five writers, several questions relate directly or indirectly to naturalism:

- "what are the differences between the language spoken by TV characters, and the language spoken by 'real' people?"
- "is there anything that's particularly common or frequent in TV dialogue, like any ways of speaking or any kinds of expressions or practices?"
- "how naturalistic do you think TV dialogue should be" (sometimes I explicitly asked if there are limits)

I also asked writers if features of spoken language such as *you know* or *like* or *well* should be used and/or to what extent they use them, for example: "do you think you should use them, these kinds of features? Like *you know, like, well*?" Sometimes I included additional examples like *yeah, um, right* in my question. In their answers, some writers referred to these kinds of linguistic devices as *handles*.

Differences between how characters speak in TV series and how people speak in "real" life

David Mandel

It's changed a lot over the last couple of years. As we've moved into these more realistic comedies, the distance between real speak and TV speak has closed. That's been the goal of television, to sound more like "real" life, that's been a striving goal. Obviously, when you're writing a comedy scene, there's a certain sort of shape – we're trying to build to the big joke – whereas when people are talking more normally, things peter out. On *Veep* in particular, one of the things we really pride ourselves on is having our script and then allowing the actors to go "you know what, let's mess it up a little bit, let's not get . . . so it's 'hi, how are you' – 'I'm fine how are you', but rather mess it up so that it is more like "real" life, so it's like 'Hi! Hey! how are you' and we're all talking all over each other and we're not just waiting for the next guy to speak". And that is part of our goal – that is something perhaps that Lucy and Ricky on *I Love Lucy* couldn't do, back in the day. So I do think it's getting closer and closer. I still think that in a lot of the multi-camera sitcoms in front of a live audience people go out of their way to say what the story is and there's a lot of text, whereas most normal human interactions are filled with subtext. So that's probably a difference that's still there; that when you're trying to move a story along, you are concerned with plot and reminding the audience of things that perhaps if you're sitting with your friends, you don't necessarily worry about, for example reminding them who the person you're talking about is.

But it's getting closer and closer, and a lot of it started with *Seinfeld*, which was obviously a very brilliant show for a lot of different reasons. There was perhaps still a little bit of that standard sitcom "you talk – I talk – you talk – I talk". However, that was where you really started to see the notion of "we're going to talk the way idiot friends at a diner talk". We're going to make fun of things, we're going to have funny names, we're going to make fun of each other, and we're going to have our own rhythms and our own words for things. And that's important to point out: that was a real beginning of the transformation of TV.

Doris Egan

Language spoken by TV characters is quite often in full sentences. There's a lot of talking around things in "real" life and broken-up sentences, even when you're not interrupted by somebody. And there are a lot of things like *um*. I remember when I was a child they had transcripts of Richard Nixon; apparently he had recorded a lot of things in the White House. And when you looked at those transcripts there was a lot of "umming" and broken sentences, and I thought, "this is what people sound like!" For some reason we don't really hear it when we're listening to people because we're in the moment. But simply writing things in full sentences – you're already taking a layer of reality away. And people also get to the point [in TV series] a lot faster because time is limited. And of course, they will often phrase things in a much better way than you would [in "real" life]. There is also a fair amount of *l'esprit de l'escalier* – staircase wit – that phenomenon when you're leaving a party and you think, "I know what I should have said to him!" Well, the writer's had quite a bit of time to think about what one character should say to the other, and they can say it in the moment. So you have the benefit of all that. In fact, even dialogue that is supposedly realistic is not true-to-life realism, it's really more of a way of defining . . . for lack of a better word I'll call it a "genre". But it's not going to be *cinéma vérité*.

Sheila Lawrence

A lot of it depends on the type of television show that you're writing on, certainly. I would say that you definitely want the dialogue to come across as realistic, as the way people speak. But truthfully, if you look at a transcript of the way people speak, it doesn't always sound great. People repeat the same idea over and over in slightly different words, or start a sentence and stop it, or just say stupid arguments or things that just don't make sense. So it's like giving characters the trappings of casual sounding dialogue but done better. And I would say, a lot of times when you turn in a script and you get notes back on it, people might actually give you the note "make this messier, mess it up a little bit, it's sounding too written". And I think that's kind of what I'm talking about, about finding the balance, between wanting it to sound the way we imagine people sound, but not be quite as ineloquent as people often are in "real" life.

Robert Berens

The characters speak in TV because they're serving a narrative to a certain point, or their language tends to be more directed. And in "real" life, conversations are circular, they have detours, they stray from the main point, and there are ways to represent that even in scripted dialogue. But you don't go as far in that direction in scripted dialogue or the scene loses its energy, because dramatically a scene needs to be about more or less one thing. And real dialogue tends to ramble or move all over the place. I think this transcript will prove that dialogue can be a little rambling and discursive and dramatically you can't do that. That said, there are ways to indicate in dialogue, to sort of cheat or sub for that: you can have characters have incomplete thoughts, you can have them stop and start a little bit. There are indications for that in scripts, to represent to the audience but also to represent maybe even to the actor that you want that line of dialogue to be spoken as if it's something they're struggling towards, because that's how you make it more dramatic, how you make it more interesting. A flat line of dialogue like the idea just popped fully formed into someone's head would be depicted as a single clear sentence. But for one, that might have more of a halting discovery feel, you might put some stops and starts. You might indicate in an action line: you might say "haltingly" or "they're realizing" or find ways to indicate different kinds of expression.

Jane Espenson

I love this question – I have thought about this my whole career. For one example, I have tried to make my television characters stop calling each other by their names, because it is a very weird thing that doesn't happen as much in "real" life. The problem is, the rhythm calls for it. There is a rhythm to dialogue writing where there's music to it and the words are the lyrics. There's this rhythm, and you need to make a thing sink in, so sometimes you need the punctuation of a person's name. And because every character on TV does that, it feels a little weird without it.

Also, when you're writing a pilot for a new show and all the characters are new, or you're interviewing a guest star on a show, you want to make sure that everybody knows who's being referred to, so you want to make sure the viewer's heard the name a couple times. So this is a rare time where you actually *do* want to think about the viewers and put that name in.

Still, I try to avoid it. I try to cut it when I can and find other ways to convey the characters' names or jobs or relationships. Instead of giving a name or saying "as district attorney, I . . ." or "as your sister . . .", I try to do it in a subtler way like having one character say to another "dad says hi" which tells you that they're siblings (although now people are sort of catching on to that). A voiceover is also an easy crutch, just telling the audience everything about the character's relationships. So it's better, classier, to try and find ways using dialogue that are less obvious.

I also find that when a character asks another character a question, I often will have that character say *yes* or *no* and then elaborate. And then when I'm polishing it [the script], I'll usually take the *yes* or *no* out, because the explanation that follows tells you whether it's *yes* or *no*, and just duplicates the *yes* or *no*, but in a more interesting and dynamic way. So I'll cut that out.

While I think a real person would say the *yes* or *no*, I find with TV characters it's better if they don't.

Another thing, not strictly about the naturalness of dialogue, but about where and when that dialogue is spoken: when characters enter a scene, they often have to react to the previous scene, even though they would have talked about it in the cab on the way over. Characters will often enter the scene going like "well, that was an embarrassing dinner party" and you're like "you were just theoretically all in a cab together for like 20 minutes!" On *Survivor*, an unscripted reality TV show, they are clearly told that they cannot discuss what happened at tribal council until they get back to camp, because there's always a shot of them all walking away from tribal council; then the next episode starts with them setting aside their torches when they arrive back at camp and saying "oh my god, could you believe it!" They clearly have not been allowed to talk on the walk. And what we're doing in scripted shows is just like that and it's very weird in both instances, because people don't do that. But a cab is an extra set and the back-home set is a standing set, so it's easier. So I had a boss once who wrote on the white-board "what did they talk about in the cab?", because he wanted to avoid that. He would find ways to make it clear that characters had already been talking about it, or to put the scene in the cab and cover it there. Other shows just own it, because you know TV audiences will just accept it. There is a thing called an "ice box question", also called a "hey May": that's when you're like "this isn't how it would really happen, but the audience isn't going to notice until after the episode's over and they're at the ice box making a sandwich". And they call that "hey May, did you wonder why they didn't talk about that in the cab?" You can tell that's an old TV term because "ice box" is a term for "refrigerator" that hasn't been around for a long time. But it's whatever you go do after the show and then you think "wait, did that actually make sense?"

I can come up with more examples, because this strikes me all the time – "a person wouldn't say that" – if something comes out too perfect. And I think there is something so powerful in the spoken mistake that you can allow a character to make. Because every writer is always thinking about subtext. How do I let the audience know what this character is thinking without them just saying it? One of the most powerful ways is to have them start to say it and then pull themselves back. So they say "I just really wanted to say how . . . how much I . . . how glad I am that you came here today". You know what they were going to say. They didn't say it. And now the audience knows what they're thinking. And, since it went by so fast, the audience may not even know why they know what they're thinking. It's really powerful and I don't think it's used enough. Let the characters make mistakes!

What uses of language are especially common in TV dialogue?

David Mandel

There's a couple of things that happen with TV dialogue that you have to remember: number one: TV dialogue has the value of the edit room, which is to say, I'll go through and I'll pull out annoying pauses and *ums* and *uhs* and whatnot, and sometimes people will in normal talk perhaps repeat something as you're trying to find a thought, and those kinds of things. However, with the wonders of editing I can go through and I can take a lot of that out and tighten it up. So, in a weird way, TV talk is often smoother just because I can take that struggle out in an edit room.

I think television is very taken, perhaps more than "real" life, with a combination of similes, metaphors, and euphemisms. That's where television perhaps strives to go; for example, on a network where we can't say *fuck you* we're going to come up with a more elaborate way of saying *fuck you*, without saying *fuck you*. Or even on a show like *Veep* where we *can* say *fuck you*, we're going to try and create a more elaborate way of saying *fuck you*, because we want to create an ornate or a rich language. Also, in general, despite our desire to sound like the way regular people talk, there is a premium placed on coming up with a metaphor that a really smart person might come up with – but more regularly than perhaps a smart person might come up with one. Instead of just saying "oh he's tired", I can go "well he's as tired as a . . . something witty". It's a little more complicated, because it's entertainment and it's television.

Doris Egan

Names. Names are notorious and some people hate the use of names. I don't care, I'm fine with names. They can add a certain rhythm to things, and of course there are always times during certain sorts of arguments when I see no realistic problem with using names. But I remember one of the formative shows I watched before I started writing for television was *The X Files*. And it was always "Mulder, Mulder, Mulder", every other line. And I'm like, "they're sitting right next to each other!" But I didn't mind. It was just part of the rhythm of the back-and-forth between them. And I almost feel like that's one of those things that someone made a rule about because it didn't seem realistic, but to me it's an artificial rule. It's just a matter of whether you're okay with it or not and I don't mind it.

The only other thing that immediately comes to mind – and this is just used sometimes, but I find it actually a very useful thing – is when one of the characters says to the other, "So what you're *really* saying is . . . ". You can then encapsulate it for the audience, which can actually be very useful, and quite often it can either be done in a funny way, or it can be an argument, which is another great way of getting information out to the audience. So that's actually another trick that I don't mind.

Sheila Lawrence

The word *like* has been overused a lot in recent years. It's an easy go-to to make something sound less written, to make it sound as if the character's having to think. "Like . . . blah blah blah". It casualizes it. I think the *likes* and *you knows*, those kinds of things are used a lot in writing dialogue right now. I feel like *guys* – as in *hey guys* – is incredibly overused. Not just in scripted TV but also in talk shows. It's become this weird shortcut to convey a friendship even with someone you don't know or a casualness or a relationship with someone you don't even know, like "hey guys! Guys! Guys!" It's everywhere.

Robert Berens

I think terseness, just generally, like catchphrases and stuff. Most conversations don't reach such clear, simple declarative statements but in TV, you'll put a dialogue button on a scene to indicate it's done and a character will take charge of the scene and say, "we'll get it done". Statements like that which I think are common tropes of TV writing. I think that if someone said that to you in "real" life you would laugh at them, because it's a little absurd in "real" life.

What else? In general I would say the ratio of jokes maybe . . . and there's a glibness that creeps in. You know, jokes are a great way to cloak exposition even in dramatic television so that it's not just bare functional dialogue. So banter and that witty wise-cracking thing I don't think operates at the same level or in the same way as jokes expressed in "real" life do. Certainly, human conversation can be very, very funny and people can be very, very funny in their day-to-day, but the corners on that are not as sharp or not as directed towards punch lines as they are in script and dialogue.

Jane Espenson

My friend Brad Bell, a very good writer whom I have partnered with, noticed a thing in my writing. He said "you know what you do, you have a character say 'here's the thing'". And it's true! I've tried to wean myself off it. For example, when a character starts grappling with the theme, grappling with what has been their genuine motivation for the whole script, and now we're in act five and we're having our emotional resolution and they say "you know what I've learned". Nobody does that anymore – nobody does the "I think we've all learned something here". But we mark it in other ways, and one of the ways we mark it is something like "here's the thing".

But there are other ways: if you want a character to say something important, to build up to that moment, to let that moment live on a pedestal, uninterrupted by anybody else so it really lands. If, say, Giles on *Buffy* is ramping into a big moment, you might write "Giles stops, takes off his glasses, polishes them, then looks up, his eyes bright", says his important dialogue, then there's another stage direction saying, like, "Buffy thinks about that". So you've just set that little piece of dialogue all alone by itself between two little clumps of stage direction. And this isn't just a pagination or paragraph issue of how it looks on the page. When the actor speaks, they're saying a line that's been set off and isolated from the other lines with bits of business, and they know to give it that prominence in their performance. So you do that kind of trick all the time, thinking "how does this moment not get lost in a little block of dialogue in the middle of a page". And I've done things in some scripts where I've even bolded a line. But you do any trick you can think of to make that really crucial line stand out. And that can include linguistic markers like "here's the thing" or "here's what I've learned", which is a really stupid one. But something like that does you the service of telling the audience "here's the moment where the character gets real". By the way, a parenthetical I use more than probably any other is "genuine". If I want that actor to know this line is what you really think, or you're lying really well, I'll put "genuine".

How naturalistic should TV dialogue be?[3]

David Mandel

I do think there are limits. For example, I could take a 55-minute show and I can go through and tighten up some of the pauses, the *ahs* and the *uhs* and whatnot, and I might get two minutes out. In editing time, if I'm trying to get to under 30 minutes, that's a very precious two minutes. Obviously, in life we don't have those time limits. So there is a value in that. On the same token, I'm the first to point out that there are times where I'll go, "you know what, that character's trying to think of that thought, let's leave in that stutter because I think that shows the stutter". But it is a slightly more idealized version of our everyday speak, and that's why we are still on the journey to the more, if you will, perfect version of "real" life dialogue. But there are newer shows that pride themselves on realism. *Louie*, the Louis CK show, might be an example of a show that is perhaps a little less concerned with punch lines and whatnot as some other comedies, and perhaps in the name of realism is willing to play some of the silences or things of that nature, and maybe even some of the stutters. So again it depends a little bit on the show. On *Veep*, we're definitely trying for that level of realism, but at the same time, we're also still trying for the big punch lines. That being said, even in the way we will cut a scene we try not to specifically end a scene with just the joke and then cut to the next scene. Often we'll do a joke, then allow the characters to break up naturally, which is approximating what real conversation might be like. I don't think we're necessarily perfectly there, but it's an attempt at what we think real conversations are like. So again better than it was, but not perfect.

Sheila Lawrence

I think it does need to reflect the way people speak. But I do think if it's in terms of just mirroring the way people talk – messy sentences, repeating the same idea over and over and over – then no, that's not entertaining. At the end of the day, it still has to be entertaining and the way a lot of people speak in "real" life isn't.

Robert Berens

I think it depends on the show, and I think there are shows where that's what you're watching for and then there are shows that if you attempted to introduce it, that would cut against the whole project in a way. So I think, in general, genre TV, or network television tends towards a kind of stylization or concision or artifice even. That said, there's a way in which naturalism is as much a style as network sitcom style. It's just the other end of the same pole. But they're all style choices. So I don't think I have a hard favorite. I think it's about, for what show you're writing, finding the right balance or approach in terms of naturalism or stylization.

Jane Espenson

I think it's important for screenwriters to have the ear of a linguist, to hear what people are really saying and write it down, which helps the actors say what people really say. Hearing an actor struggle to say *shouldn't have*, with every syllable perfect, nobody needs that, nobody says that, so why make them try to say it? I write *shouldn't've* every time. My ideal is writing how people talk, but with that little bit more structure – and heightened. I think that with pure verisimilitude you do run the risk of losing some drama.

"Real" life is a bit lacking in beautiful structure. That's why I don't use the *goodbye*s on the phone in a script. The *goodbye*s are total realism but they don't earn their place. "Real" life is messy and horrible and unstructured. We can present something that is wittier, that we can aspire to – that life should have more thoughtful, more literary speech.

But I think different shows value different things. Sorkin dialogue is different than Whedon dialogue is different than Sherman-Palladino dialogue. But they would all say they're there to do different things. There are shows that aren't in the business of holding a mirror up to life. They don't mind if it looks artificial, because they are creating a specific kind of object to show the audience. Other shows that are more interested in looking like life, like *Gilmore Girls*, will keep in mind things like that people joke in a tragic situation. If you want to sound like life, if that is the goal, to hold the mirror up to life, then your dialogue should have some humor in it.

One of the first scripts I wrote for *Battlestar Galactica* had a teaser set in the hanger deck, and when Ron [Moore] rewrote it, it came out full of dual dialogue. Dual dialogue is when you have dialogue going in two columns to indicate the characters are overlapping. And it was beautiful. It sounded like "real" life, people talking over each other, and it was okay if you don't catch every word. We, in "real" life, can hear two things said at once pretty well if there's not a lot of difficult stuff, like doing math, going on. I can hear that guy's yelling *hey Joe*, while I'm talking to you. And Ron took that and made it chaotic and beautiful and I was like "oh okay, this is a song I can sing at this show". Other shows don't want that, they want every word to be heard – every word is given its little moment in the sun. That was one of the things I loved about *Battlestar*: that you got to play with overlapping dialogue where you might not catch every word but you get the gist of what's being said, and you get that sense of a chaotic situation. So I used the dual dialogue function in [screenwriting software] Final Draft more in *Battlestar Galactica* than I ever have before or since. In *Once Upon a Time* we don't tend to do that. You might have someone chanting a spell in the background and use double dialogue, very rarely, but it's just not a show that works that way.

To what extent do you script words and phrases like *you know, like, well, yeah, right*?

David Mandel

Sometimes those handles are very necessary. In fact, there are times where we've added *wells* or *Madam Presidents* or something; maybe it's to smooth over something, or just a new thought came up that even though it was real, it was so jarring that it felt like it needs a conversational handle of adding in "well, I think" as opposed to just "I think". So they serve their place, but any time you can, tighten it up into an idealized form. That's the realities of a show as opposed to worrying obsessively about language.

Doris Egan

I don't use them a lot. I will sometimes use them in the course of one person speaking, if it speaks to who they are. And I'll do it almost rhythmically the same way I would use *fucking* as an adjective for a certain character, like "get your fucking elbow off that fucking table", and might add *yeah* or an *uh,* as part of getting the rhythm of a particular character down. I don't do it as a normal thing even though in "real" life we reinforce each other with that sort of thing. And in fact, there was an actress who is always making these kind of sighs and nodding and whatnot – a fine actress whom everyone loves deeply, and I will not mention her name even though I'm saying everyone loved her, as did I, but that one habit of hers drove me a little crazy – and whenever possible I hope we're not going to see that in editing because it was just distracting. So I would say if you don't notice it consciously in "real" life, you probably don't want to put it with malice aforethought into your script.

Sheila Lawrence

If you were writing a medical show, you wouldn't want a doctor speaking with a lot of *likes*. But if you're writing a group of 20-year-olds sitting around in their apartment, then I think it is an accurate reflection. Given that that is the way a lot of people speak, it probably wouldn't feel genuine to an audience if you didn't write it like that.

Robert Berens

That's interesting, because I tend to use those a lot. And I consider our dialogue in its way very stylized, but I think you work those in because they're very helpful. And you limit your dialogue by not including those things. I almost need to have access to those to write, because that's how we speak. And shy of having someone speak in a rhetorically circular way, which I think is generally a bridge too far in drama, to represent an argument that doesn't go from point A to point B but instead wanders off-point, that would be naturalism taken past the point of acceptable dramatization. But in the actual diction and syntax incorporating naturalistic touches like that I think is thoroughly essential, because it's flavor. Bare dialogue that's just expressing the point is boring, it's not interesting. It's certainly not fun to write, and I don't think it's fun to watch. That said, not to keep bringing up qualifications, but depending on how a show operates, there are shows where the dialogue is actually laid down fairly functionally and cleanly, because the expectation is that the actors are going to bring that flavor, that they will have that freedom whether it's through improvization or whatever to bring that, to give that spin to the dialogue.

Jane Espenson

They tend to be minimized, because characters sound weird when they do them, because it's not how TV characters traditionally have been written. If you put in a lot of those it just doesn't sound like normal TV speak. And there's a deeper problem, which is that it is very hard for actors to convincingly put in the pauses, *you knows*, all those little markers, in a way that sounds extremely natural when they are being told where to put them. If you want that feeling in your dialogue, a better practice is to tell the actors "you can say it how it comes out of your mouth most naturally, you can put those in, put them in where they feel natural to you".

But some shows don't work like that. On *Buffy*, the actors really weren't encouraged to put in stuff like that, on *Battlestar*, they were very much encouraged to. If you listen to the two shows, that's part of how they sound different. If you listen to *Buffy*, I think you can hear that every word, every syllable is there because Joss [Whedon] wanted it there. Ron Moore on *Battlestar* was like "however you want to say it, or say something totally different, we'll work with it!" It was very much top-down versus bottom-up, and the shows sound different as a result. Joss's shows sound more polished, almost in a literal way – a polished object where every bit of the sculpture is where you wanted it. And Ron Moore's more like the kinetic sculpture where it's moving around and it's not always planned. I think the Ron Moore way feels more realistic, but the Joss way often feels funnier, because comedy relies on precision. I suppose it's a trade-off.

One other thought, before we more away from *you know*. There's a term called "handles", I haven't heard it in drama but I have heard it in sitcoms a lot, which is the *well* at the beginning of a sentence or *you know* or *I mean*. A lot of times, those would end up in the script because, particularly in half-hour writing, the process of writing is as verbal as the performance of it: you are coming up with a line and then shouting it out and then it gets typed in. So you naturally get those handles in half-hour writing. And then when your script comes in long and you need to take a page out, you go and remove all the handles. So you are purposefully removing a natural feature of spoken English to pull up a page, in the theory that by removing all of those you are actually making the episode shorter. Although the fraction of a second that's spent on the *I mean* is clearly negligible, for the network-consoling feature of having one page less in scripting, we'll sacrifice the handles, and I think that's a mistake, but one I have made. I have often made a line worse, less idiomatic, in order to pull up a page.

Summary and advice

As the interviewees state, TV dialogue is not and cannot be fully naturalistic or realistic. Some of the key differences that these writers mention include the way the talk between speakers is structured (*turn-taking*), with fewer broken or incomplete sentences, mistakes, overlapping speech, repetitions, and so on. Pauses, repetitions, hesitations, and phrases such as *you know*, *like*, or *well* can get scripted by writers for particular functions (for example, creating realism or revealing character aspects such as age or emotion), but they can also be included by actors in their performance, and, conversely, they can be removed in the edit room. In addition, several of the writers point to variation between particular series and Bob Berens calls naturalism and stylization "style choices".

One conclusion we can draw from this is that it is important to know what type of dialogue you are aiming to write – *where* it is located on the scale from stylization to naturalism. And if you do want your dialogue to be more "naturalistic", avoid using TV dialogue clichés, catchphrases, directly addressing the audience, and so on. Instead, try using some of these features of naturally occurring conversation:

- characters speaking at the same time (overlapping) or interrupting each other
- characters making mistakes, hesitating, speaking in incomplete sentences or correcting themselves or changing the topic
- characters using some "handles" at the beginning of lines or "fillers" within lines – this includes words and expressions like *actually, you know, I mean, like*, and many others
- characters using signals at the end of lines that indicate their turn is over (for example, *know what I'm saying, know what I mean*)
- characters hesitating when they speak (*um, uh . . .*) and providing minimal one-word cues that they are listening while other characters are speaking (*mmm, uh-huh, yeah . . .*)

But beware that these features are not just randomly used in conversation. To make sure that you are using these conversational characteristics realistically, you could record and analyze a conversation with your friends (ask them for consent first!). To find out more about the limits of naturalistic dialogue in fictional television, analyze a few conversations from a

TV series that uses such a style so that you do not overuse these features. (Alternatively, you could indicate some of these features through an action line or parenthetical and leave it up to the actor to bring in the "messiness", as noted by the writers above as a possibility for some series.)

Another insight from these interviews is that the five writers nominated different uses of language as especially common in TV dialogue, rather than all interviewees listing the same words and expressions. My own computer-based analysis of language use in US TV dialogue shows that the following words and expressions are among those that are frequent in TV series:

> *alright, well, look, sorry, come on, don't worry, out of here, oh my god, what . . . are you doing, what are you doing here, why don't you . . ., I need you to . . ., what . . . are you talking about, what are you going to/gonna do, wh*-word *(what, why . . .) the hell*, the names and nicknames of characters

You may want to *use* these and other common words and expressions so that your dialogue sounds like "typical" TV dialogue – or you may want to *avoid* using them so that your dialogue sounds fresher, more innovative. These uses of language also have particular functions. For example, character names, nicknames, and identifying labels (*sister, doctor, detective*, . . .) are useful for introducing and identifying characters, but, as mentioned by Doris Egan above, they tend to be overused in TV series.

Notes

1 In the foreword to Paulo Quaglio, *Television Dialogue: The Sitcom Friends vs. Natural Conversation* (Amsterdam/Philadelphia: John Benjamins, 2009).
2 See for example Chapter 4 in Kay Richardson, *Television Dramatic Dialogue: A Sociolinguistic Study* (Oxford: Oxford University Press, 2010), and Chapter 10 in Monika Bednarek, *Language and Television Series: A Linguistic Approach to TV Dialogue* (Cambridge: Cambridge University Press, 2018).
3 Doris Egan's answer is not provided here, as she discussed this previously under *Differences between how characters speak in TV series and how we speak in "real" life*.

References

Bednarek, Monika. *Language and Television Series: A Linguistic Approach to TV Dialogue*. Cambridge: Cambridge University Press, 2018.

Quaglio, Paulo. *Television Dialogue: The Sitcom Friends vs. Natural Conversation*. Amsterdam/Philadelphia: John Benjamins, 2009.

Richardson, Kay. *Television Dramatic Dialogue. A Sociolinguistic Study*. Oxford: Oxford University Press, 2010.

5 On the expression of emotion

Introductory remarks

When we examine how language is used in television series it is clear that emotionality is key. For example, words or phrases that express emotion are highly important and occur more frequently in TV dialogue than in data from "real" life conversations.[1] Some examples include evaluative adjectives like *crazy*, *beautiful*, *wrong*, emotion words like *hurt*, *love*, and *worry*, swear or taboo words like *bitch, crap,* or *hell*, and words like *honey*, which characters use to address each other affectionately. Such emotionality is very important for creating dramatic and captivating stories that engage viewers and make them care about the characters.

Screenwriting manuals also emphasize emotional aspects of televisual stories, which are important for driving story and engaging the audience.[2] But how can we use language – as opposed to the actor's performance – to signal character emotion to the audience? In my interviews, I asked variants of the following question: "how can you express a character's emotion through the dialogue in particular? How would you convey that this character now feels a specific emotion?"

David Mandel

In television world, we're looking for subtext. So if a character's in a bad mood I try and think to my own life. What do I do if I'm in a bad mood? I might pick a fight with somebody, or I might be bothered by things that shouldn't bother me normally. So I'm trying to build a certain amount of agitation into my dialogue; I'm creating a situation. So I might have a character go "can you please move away, can you back up", to try and express some level of annoyance with the main person and that character. That's some of the ways to do that.

You might have a character, an upset character, a depressed character: we did a depression scene this season on *Veep*, and we had the character complaining incessantly about the food choices and how ultimately she really hated all of the food from everywhere and every place, instead of just going "I'm depressed". There's a reality side to it when nothing makes you happy. It was funny at the same time, which obviously for us is important, which is to say to see a character complaining about hating every kind of food, but ultimately it's a way of expressing that there's something off about this character. So those choices are very particular.

Doris Egan

It depends on what that emotion is. If characters are angry, it is almost always useful to provoke them, particularly if there's information that can come out. Because that's something the audience enjoys – when a character unloads, particularly if they can do so amusingly even if they're angry; they want to hear it all come out. I personally find if it's something about love, for instance, the less said the better. It should be said, in that case, without words, by a gesture – and I don't mean a kiss – or by a back-and-forth. Here's what I mean by back-and-forth where they're not stating what they're thinking, and I'll use *House* as an example, and that was about friendship. There's an episode where House and Wilson have a big argument and Wilson is very angry at House. And it's also the first episode where you found out that House is a rabid atheist and despises religion. It was called "House vs. God" and there was a whiteboard where House and God both had marks. And after all the arguments and after House had done some stuff to Wilson that upset him, we're at the very end and they're walking out of the hospital and House says to him, "but you and me, we're okay, right?" And Wilson gives him this disbelieving look, and he says "House, you are . . ." and then his voice changes to fond exasperation: ". . . as God made you", and then he goes away. And I even put the pause in there to let the actor know. It felt to the audience like he was about to unload on him and then instead he's sort of saying we're always going to be friends. But again it was *without* saying "we're always going to be friends" because that is death to state those things.

Sheila Lawrence

I absolutely think you can [express emotion through dialogue], it's what I tend to do. Apparently, film and television is a visual medium and you're supposed to think first about how to tell the story visually but I don't – I always think of the words first, that's just how my brain works. So there's no question to me that I would express a lot of emotion with words rather than the visual of, say, seeing someone cry. To try to describe how I would do that is where I'm tripping up a little bit. It's always very personal. For me, the process is trying to put yourself in the situation and what would I be feeling and then what would I say if I were to want to express those things that are going on inside. And once you've done that, then that's sort of the starting point I think. And then you go back and again it's that process of "would a person actually just spill all of this as lovely as maybe you've written it?" People don't always tend to put all of their emotions in their words, so then you kind of pick and choose and pull back to something that resembles reality a little bit more.

There's a million examples. I think of things where characters are fighting over something so incredibly insignificant and you know that it is absolutely about something else. In one writers' room we used to always call that the turkey sandwich, that people are fighting over – you know, the wife made a turkey sandwich the way the husband doesn't like it or whatever. But what they're really fighting about is some issue in their marriage where they're not meeting each other's expectations. But very few people talk as directly about the real thing going on, so it plays out in day-to-day life in terms of what's actually in front of us. It's a way of getting at the emotion without saying it as blatantly as "I'm angry at you", which in "real" life a lot of us don't do.

Robert Berens

Some of it [the emotion] you outsource to the action lines, the sort of narrative framework. So you're indicating it, but you're leaving it out of the wording. But you find ways to indicate that haltingness or something: you can use ellipses or double dashes to cut off thoughts, to indicate moments at which they've maybe reached the unsayable, because it's too emotionally overwhelming. So you do an ellipsis or a double dash to indicate. If there's a statement that's almost too direct or melodramatic, but you want to get the intense emotion, you bring the person right up to the point of expressing something, but they don't actually say it, which is a completely effective way to convey the emotion without being as saccharine as just blurting it. And relatedly, it's finding the moments where they don't say the thing.

[On whether more implicit ways are more important than explicitly saying "I hate you" or "I love you"]

It's interesting that you say that because in this script I have an "I hate you" in there. And hopefully that moment is going to play right and it's going to be the right expression. But for me this is a case where in my opinion I'm paying off twelve years of story in that line of dialogue. And it's such an about-face from our understanding of what he thought, but at the same time when he says it we realize he means it. So there's a lot of context building up to that "I hate you" that makes something so simple and painful. And it's so shocking for him to realize, because it's a moment of realization. It's not just two characters who have been in conflict, "I hate you, you jerk, buzz off". It's the person I've been engaged in this thing with, like "I have deep hatred for this person and I didn't even realize it". So I think that it's not one or the other, it's about the moments when it's right to be elliptical and the moments when it's right to just land that direct thing.

Jane Espenson

[To express emotion] you usually don't want a character to just come right out and say it. So I often use the aborted sentence or the backtrack to suggest subtext. And, of course, you have to think about all the tricks that you use in "real" life when you can't just come out and say something. If someone knows that his wife is overhearing him, he can't just say to his friend, "hey, I can't talk to you now, because she's here". So what does he say instead? Well, he's going to employ all the same tricks that a screenwriter uses to convey the things their characters just can't blurt out. I mean, this is the joy of screenwriting. Where I thrive, and where I think a lot of us thrive, is the working out of problems like "okay, what would I say that would tell someone that there's something I'm not saying?"

Summary and advice

While emotionality can be established in non-dialogue sections of the script (action lines or parentheticals) or in the actor's performance, dialogue is also used by writers to indicate that a character has a particular emotional response. The five screenwriters mention relatively indirect ways of expressing emotional responses: for instance, bringing characters to the point of saying something and then cutting them off, using aborted sentences or backtracking, or complaining/nit-picking to show that a character is depressed. They also mention more direct (and seemingly less preferred) ways of expressing emotion such as *I hate you* or *jerk*.

Often, the expression of emotion through dialogue seems to be created by these writers intuitively and imaginatively. We can unpack this a little by looking at how people express emotions in "real" life. There are many different ways in which this happens through language,[3] and we can find these ways in TV dialogue, too: characters can name or label an emotion (*I'm so happy*; *I love you; I hate him; I detest X; X upset me; I can't stand it when . . .*; *I don't trust him*; *such a surprise!*) or mention emotional (physical) behavior (*I was laughing so hard . . .; you're making me cry; don't shout at me!*). Character emotions can also be expressed by:

- using interjections (*whoa; hey; wow; ugh; aw; oh man; oh my goodness . . .*) or swear/taboo words (*bitch; crap; damn; hell; fuck; shit . . .*)
- using emphasis and intensification (*I'm so sorry; I totally fucked up; seriously . . .*)
- using imperatives or exclamations (*oh come on! Stop right now! How dare he! . . .*)
- using adjectives that express an attitude (*best, crazy, beautiful, wrong . . .*)
- using repetition (*really really really; no no no no! . . .*)
- using pet names (*honey, sweetie, darling, buddy . . .*) or insults/derogatory labels (*you're an asshole . . . ; what a jerk . . . ; this shithole . . .*)
- hesitating, interrupting oneself or someone else, and other "dysfluencies" (signaling nervousness, emotional turmoil, anger . . .)

These are just some of the many ways in which language can express a character's emotion. Of course, this always depends on the specific emotion that is expressed, especially whether that emotion is positive (like joy, love) or negative (like anger, sadness). If you get the chance, you can unobtrusively observe how you and others express their emotions through language – or you can record and analyze how characters express their emotions in TV series.

Notes

1 Monika Bednarek, *Language and Television Series: A Linguistic Approach to TV Dialogue* (Cambridge: Cambridge University Press, 2018), 140–144.
2 Monika Bednarek, *Language and Television Series: A Linguistic Approach to TV Dialogue* (Cambridge: Cambridge University Press, 2018), 211, 273 (Chapter 10, note 2).
3 See for example the overview in Monika Bednarek, *Emotion Talk across Corpora* (Houndmills/New York: Palgrave Macmillan, 2008).

References

Bednarek, Monika. *Emotion Talk across Corpora*. Houndmills/New York: Palgrave Macmillan, 2008.

Bednarek, Monika. *Language and Television Series: A Linguistic Approach to TV Dialogue*. Cambridge: Cambridge University Press, 2018.

6 On building characters through language

Introductory remarks

Viewers are drawn into stories through characters, take interest in what happens to them, and engage with them emotionally. Characters and their goals are regarded as central to televisual stories, to the extent that some advice states "story *is* character".[1] No doubt many other aspects contribute to establishing characters, but how can we do this through writing dialogue? To find out what writers think, I asked them "how do you build a character's personality or individuality through language?"

David Mandel

I think there's three pieces involved in this. Obviously there is the language, there is who the character is, and in a lot of cases there's who the actor is. Oftentimes parts (acting roles) are a little bit like a suit or a dress that you might buy off the rack, and then in a perfect world it'd be altered and tailored to get everything just right. And that's the difference: when the right actor can have their part. So you're testing out your part because that actor has truths that you think affect that part and now you have that right combo, you have a sense of who this character is.

For example, on *Veep* there's the character Kent, played by Gary Cole, he's a statistics and numbers guy, very scientific. One of the things we've learned about him over the years is he's funnier but also to the point of him sometimes just saying one word. Often it's the word correcting you, so sometimes it's another character saying something and then him simply saying one word – it might be the word that either corrects your grammar or your pronunciation, or a fact or something like that, but again just the comedy of the one word along with the correction gives full bore to this character. On the flipside, he will often have explanations of very cold, esoteric facts, and those will often be longer, but again we're looking for very specific, scientific, number language in there. And we'll go on the internet, we'll call mathematician friends whatnot, to try and make sure we're getting some real words in there, and often he's doing this so that another character can then make fun of him, and we definitely play into those things with the language choices. At the same time, if that's all we did, it would be a little bit boring, so we also pepper this character with likes and dislikes. So, for example, over the years we've discovered he's a *Grateful Dead* fan; once he'd written a romance novel; we've seen that he rides a motorcycle. Those things all come together and build this character.

On the flipside, there's a character Kevin Dunn plays, which is Ben, the chief of staff. He's been there forever, seen everything, slow moving – he moves because he wants to move. Kevin, the actor, is incredibly dry, and the character is well mirrored, and those things come together very nicely. And so we look to him for certain truths and hard analysis, as we're trying to put words in his mouth: he's often the most biting, reductive – being able to analyze a situation and reduce it to something. And you do start to find "that is a Ben line, that is a Kevin line".

Doris Egan

This is the sort of thing I was thinking of when I was mentioning a character who would say "get your fucking elbows off the fucking table". I mean, you get class, background, education, you can get a certain level of the kind of character who's always angry, you can get a lot of that just from the rhythm of their dialogue. You can't work miracles, but I do think the rhythm of their dialogue and the way they express themselves will have a lot to do with how much the audience likes them. And by that I don't mean because they are within their world a likeable character, but if they're for example a character who says what they think without regard to anybody or anything, the audience will enjoy it because that's sort of a fantasy that people have and no one actually does. And if they can accomplish that amusingly, the audience will love them. So to an extent you can make a character popular through just the way they say things. But I'm going to be ruthlessly honest and say for 90% of television it doesn't matter that much as long as the dialogue is not bad and it hits all its marks and it tells the story – most of the time that will be okay.

Sheila Lawrence

It's difficult [to build personality through the dialogue], but I personally find it very important. I find it troubling when every character on the page speaks in the same voice. Back in the '90s, the problem I had with a lot of sitcoms I worked on was that if one character had more jokes than another character, they would just say "oh well, give Joe two of Bob's lines" and that's all very wrong to me. How are we not able to distinguish people by their voices, by the words that they use? That doesn't seem like very good writing. So I think there are lots of ways of distinguishing characters through their language. I'm writing a character right now who rarely ever uses contractions. She is very well educated and comes from a very upper class family and doesn't slip into that. She speaks in a more proper way. There are characters who would not use the word *really* as much as I do and a lot of people do. There are characters who would say *very* and they wouldn't be a *really* or a *really, really* kind of person. And I think that conveys a certain propriety, a certain education level, a certain intellectualism, probably a certain age.

Also, I think how much characters are willing to express themselves, their forthcomingness with their language, is very telling of character. On *Desperate Housewives*, all the characters are very different but I'm not sure how much that's reflected in language as opposed to just attitude. There are things that Lynette would say that Bree would never say, but I don't think it's words used per se, it's more the idea of expressing a thought that you have, rather than keeping it inside. Gaby was a character who would say anything that was on her mind and tell people what she thought of them, and in very direct language. Bree would find a way to sugarcoat, with the very same thoughts and intent, but just with a different way verbally of going about it that to an outside ear would seem perfectly civilized, but underneath she's really being quite critical.

Robert Berens

That's a hard question. I came on the show [*Supernatural*] in its ninth season. And so I've been here four years but so much of their voice was established when I came on the show. I really think it comes from the creator of the show and it comes from the actor who is cast. And it becomes a kind of living thing through a combination of what the actor was good at, what sounded right coming out of their mouths, and what the creator intended for their voice or their diction or their background as expressed through their syntax and diction. And at a certain point, it becomes fairly set in stone where you've internalized that sense of "you just know it when you see it" – whether as a viewer of a TV show or as a writer on the show. Like, that's Dean; that's not a Dean line; that's Dean. But that's also very debatable even still to this day. It appears fixed to me, but the reality is that a line of dialogue that you think is the most Dean line could set off alarm bells on Twitter, "Dean would never say that!". So again it's a process.

It's a hard process to describe, because there's so many episodes of the show that you've seen, so you've just internalized the voice to such an extent that it isn't necessarily a conscious or willful act. It just comes, and so it's a little bit hearing it, but it's also a little bit acting it, whether or not I'm speaking out loud to check the line of dialogue which I do sometimes but not that often. But it's kind of speaking it in my head like a form of performance. And honestly, the most enjoyable part of all of this is acting on the page. In order to express a line of dialogue in a way that feels authentic to the character, feeling what they're feeling and inhabiting a construct of their consciousness as you're working. It's like playacting, it brings you back to your childhood. And it also brings you back to the pleasure of watching TV, like melodrama, and feeling like you're watching someone have this very strong emotion. At a certain point as a consumer that gets less exciting or real or electric, particularly when you work in TV, and you sort of see it as an industrial process. But then when you're writing, periodically you get these moments where you're feeling it as acutely as you did when you were the most naïve first-time consumer of entertainment. Like "oh my god I'm as sad as he is, as they're being sad on screen". When you're writing it, you're just generating it. And I know that doesn't speak to language, but to enter that emotional state is an access to the more authentic expression or the more in-character expression.

Jane Espenson

A lot of that happens at the pilot stage, which is before the staff is hired. So there's just one writer building the character in that one script. I haven't done a ton of pilot writing. I tend to only be involved in a show after the pilot exists so the characters are there. But I have definitely taken steps to try to make a character show change. There was a line I wrote for Tara on *Buffy* where they're discussing that there's a new Buffy robot and that everyone but Buffy was able to immediately tell she was a robot. And Tara says something like "she practically had *Made in Japan* stamped on her ass". And everybody looks at her because it's out of character. And she's says, "I was just trying out some salty talk". And I turned it in, and when we got to the moment when Joss [Whedon] is giving me notes on the episode he stopped at that line and he was like "what do we feel about this? It doesn't sound like Tara". And then he thought for a minute and kept it in, because it became kind of a little character moment for Tara that showed change. Characters have moments like this, where they change and grow and deepen. Dialogue is an opportunity to show this. The characters at the periphery of a show are less nuanced than the characters at the center, which is what makes them easier and more fun to write for. Anya's a lot more fun to write for than Buffy, because Buffy has to take everyone into consideration, has to be temperate. Anya can be intemperate and crazy and have this really strong point of view. Buffy's point of view has to be tempered by taking everyone into account and being a more fully-fledged person. By giving Tara a line that's different than everything she's said before, you move her towards the center, as she gets less predictable and starts to have more aspects to her personality. And so I love doing that.

One of the first lines I wrote for Cordelia [on *Buffy*] was her saying she was good at standardized tests, in total conflict with everything we knew about Cordelia. And she says "what, I can't have layers?", which I now think is a bit on the nose, but I was very proud of it at the time. I practically explicitly had her say "I'm close enough to the center of the show to have layers as a character!" So that's one way you can deepen a character: have them do something that appears out of character, have them acknowledge "hey, this is out of character but I'm growing and changing". It's maybe a little obvious, but it worked on that show at that time.

I also got to write episodes that focused on Jonathan and Andrew on *Buffy*, characters that had been very tertiary and I got to sort of go like "okay, what if we took them seriously?" After all, in "real" life no one's a tertiary character, everyone is the hero of their own story – everyone is Buffy. So when you look closely at any one character, they should have layers, like a fine croissant, there should be all these layers, lamination, butter between the dough, and we should be able to find dialogue that reflects that and have them say things that appear out of character. An out-of-character line isn't always a mistake, it's often the deepening of a character. So I try to do that. And I think some showrunners balk at that; some showrunners say "well we've established this character, they should live in this range", which is also legit. If you get every character deepening and moving towards the center, then you stop having comedic characters who can be outlandish at the edges. So it's a trade-off.

In terms of word choice, Willow's more bookwormy than Xander. Willow might say "incontrovertible!" or something that Xander would never say. In the episode [of *Buffy*] where we can hear everyone's thoughts, the fact that Cordelia's text and her subtext were the same tells you a lot about her character and I guess that's using language to do that. Or on *Once Upon a Time*, the character of Grumpy/Leroy might say something ungrammatical. That signifies that he's a miner, working class, salt of the earth; it just marks him out as that. That's a line that he could say that Prince Charming wouldn't say. So you can do that and just sort of underline what you already know about the characters.

In *Battlestar Galactica*, Roslin and the chief spoke very different. The level of refinement and education and point of view would just be totally different. But more often than not, I've been on shows where suddenly a given character can't be in this scene, and you simply reassign their lines to another character – *and it's fine*. And someone will inevitably make a joke about "the hallmark of fine writing: we're able to just give all these lines to this other character and not make any changes".

Sometimes if a female character can't be in the scene and you give their lines to a male character, or vice versa, you end up subtly rewriting them, because a writer tends to write male and female characters slightly differently due to cultural assumptions that are so deeply ingrained you don't even notice them. And you realize that suddenly the lines that sounded fine for a female character sound passive for the male character. And this is why a good exercise is to write a character with one gender and then switch it at the last minute, and see "okay, have I written this character less strong than they should be because I've written it for a woman?" Sometimes you may put in all sorts of markers to indicate that this character's female that you subconsciously were not aware of.

I have a theory that the more serious a character is, the more they are given license to make jokes. Whereas, the more trivial a character is, the more they *are* the joke. Purposefully making a joke versus just uttering a line that is a joke are two different things. So when Buffy complains about a rash on her hand that turns out to give her the clairvoyant abilities of the episode Earshot, and she says "well that's really a problem for the fine people at Lubriderm", that's a very classic sort of stand-up comic way to say a joke – "the fine people at". Nobody says that naturally, so it marks that it is a joke made on purpose. She made a joke, which tells us two things: that she's a serious character, because she can make a joke, and that she's nervous. To me when a character makes a joke, it often tells you they're nervous. So that tells us a little bit that this rash is secretly bothering her.

Sometimes when you're writing a spec pilot or a feature, you do a dream casting in your head and you cast an actor who you want to play that role, because I think hearing the voice is very important. If I were writing a *Buffy* script I'd be hearing James Marsters' voice as Spike, and I'd be writing down what he says – and he will supply his idiolect. I don't have to think about it; Spike's talking and I write it down. And I think most writers do that. I can't listen to any music when I'm writing and I met another writer who said the same thing. He said "yeah because I can't hear the characters' voices in my head" and I said "yes! That's exactly it!" It's so auditory. I'm confident if you hooked up an MRI or something to my brain you would see that the bits of my brain that are responsible for hearing are lit up when I'm writing. I'm confident I'm hearing. It feels exactly like hearing. I'm not thinking about who that character is, I'm just hearing the actor speak. Somehow my subconscious has put that all in. But I think I'm not as good as some other writers at creating vivid characters in a script with *imaginary* casting. Other people seem to be able to come up with fully-fledged characters and never actually imagine an auditory voice of them. I have to hear the auditory voice. So I tend to just transcribe dialogue, whereas a lot of people I know will really sweat and labor and rewrite their dialogue.

Summary and advice

According to the interviewed writers, characters can be built through word choice and grammar or particular ways of speaking that come to be associated with a specific character. Sheila Lawrence suggests that it is important that characters have their own unique voice, different from other characters in the series. To some extent, this process seems to be internalized so that writers can identify dialogue as a specific character's line or even hear the character's voice. The creator of the TV series, who wrote the pilot, and the actor who embodies the character are also considered as important to character building. Some of the dimensions of character mentioned by these writers include personality traits, emotions, attitude, class, and education, age, occupation, gender, and narrative roles (for example, trivial/serious character).

To create characters on the page, it can therefore be helpful to think systematically about some of the different aspects that make up a character's identity:

- their biography (history of combined experiences)
- their relationships to other characters (family, friendship, enemies, colleagues . . .)
- their emotional responses, attitudes, values, beliefs, and ideologies
- their personality traits (their habits and their personality; for example, are they intelligent, stingy, noisy, shy, confident, arrogant, witty, religious, prejudiced . . .)
- their membership in social groups (age, class, profession, ethnicity, gender, sexuality . . .)
- their role in the narrative (for example, are they the "hero" or the "villain", or a comic foil; are they a central character or not)

You can use dialogue to indicate these aspects of character. They can be revealed through the character's *own* dialogue or through the way *other* characters talk about them, and linguists have developed comprehensive analytical models to deconstruct how such characterization works.[2]

TV characters often have their own unique style or way of using language and they use this style in each episode, unless there are good reasons for not doing so (for instance, when they pretend they are someone else). A simple example for a character's unique and consistent style is the use of catchphrases. These are often words or expressions used to indicate emotion or attitude – think of Homer's *D'oh*, Sawyer's *son of a bitch* (*Lost*), or Sheldon's *bazinga* (*The Big Bang Theory*). But catchphrases are not naturalistic or realistic as Robert Berens points out (in Chapter 2), and of course it's not appropriate to use them in all series. This depends on the nature of the series and its genre (catchphrases tend to occur in conventional sitcoms).

Notes

1 Abby Finer and Deborah Pearlman, *Starting Your Television Writing Career: The Warner Bros Television Writers Workshop Guide* (Syracuse: Syracuse University Press, 2004).

2 See for example, Jonathan Culpeper, *Language & Characterisation: People in Plays & Other Texts* (London: Longman, 2001); Monika Bednarek, *The Language of Fictional Television: Drama and Identity* (London/New York: Continuum, 2010), or Kay Richardson, *Television Dramatic Dialogue: A Sociolinguistic Study* (Oxford: Oxford University Press, 2010).

References

Bednarek, Monika. *The Language of Fictional Television: Drama and Identity*. London/New York: Continuum, 2010.

Culpeper, Jonathan. *Language & Characterisation: People in Plays & Other Texts*. London: Longman, 2001.

Finer, Abby and Deborah Pearlman. *Starting Your Television Writing Career: The Warner Bros Television Writers Workshop Guide*. Syracuse: Syracuse University Press, 2004.

Richardson, Kay. *Television Dramatic Dialogue: A Sociolinguistic Study*. Oxford: Oxford University Press, 2010.

7 On swearing

Introductory remarks

In many countries like the US, the use of indecent, profane, or obscene speech in network television is regulated, either by prohibiting or by restricting it. This means that professionals who write for broadcast TV series may have to work around external restrictions that impact on their writing. At the same time, cursing or swearing can fulfill important functions for the narrative, for example allowing characters to express their emotions realistically.[1] To find out more about writers' opinions on this important area of language use, all writers were asked about their general views on the use of swearing (for example, "what is your view on the use of swearing in TV dialogue?"). All but one were explicitly asked about its functions (for example, "when you use cursing or swearing what are its functions?").

David Mandel

One of the things about *Veep* is not just the realism of language but also the realism of the world, in this case Washington DC, where cursing is very much a real part of "real" life, but also Washington DC life. So the intent to depict that level of realism and to peel back the layers of DC, you'd be at a loss if you weren't cursing. So in this case it definitely lends that sense of realism. I also think in a world where in the television news media – and maybe some of this is pre-Trump, who obviously has a bit of a potty mouth, but in previous administrations – we're always seeing these beautiful shots of our president coming off the planes and getting on the planes and sitting with world leaders. And a lot of our entertainment like *The West Wing* has placed these presidents up on pedestals, even shows like *24*, so the president is either a very good guy or almost like a movie villain character. They're very much extremes. And so it's part of the reality, the de-pedalization, seeing a president that curses, seeing a president that's foul-mouthed. In terms of the functions, I think it humanizes these characters, it adds to the realism, and then often our cursing is very elaborately, almost incredibly written, very writer-y. They're cursing in a way that perhaps no person would actually curse given the chance. And so that is one of the conceits of the show, that it takes pride in its cursing, and in this case the pride in the cursing is an attempt at saying "this is a window into these characters' souls, they're not just cursing". But then they're in some ways so horrible that they are so good at cursing. This is the conceit. So that's one of the things we use cursing for, which obviously is not how every show does it.

Doris Egan

[Swearing has] two main functions. One is a kind of rhythm of speech, which is telling you about the background and the attitude toward something. But there are very rare occasions when a character would use a word you're not supposed to use on television, where that's the word they *would* use and almost anything else sounds odd. I did a pilot in which people land on Mars and it was done in a semi-realistic way. And there was a group that got to Mars ahead of them but this is their first time, some of the first people who have ever been on Mars. They step outside and there are a few seconds when they just have to take in the fact, and one of them says, awed, "we're on another fucking planet!" And we got a note "they can't say fucking". The thing is, you wouldn't say, "we're on another damn planet, George!" I mean they would use something big, something outside the ordinary to go with an outside-the-ordinary experience. But you aren't allowed to do that. So on the rare occasions where you're in that situation, it feels a little false if you're writing for network television because it's false, it just is. In fact, I knew when I wrote "we're on another fucking planet" someone was going to ask me along the way to change that, but I wanted to convey to everybody what this moment was before we changed it, so the actors would understand and could do their best with whatever we came up with to replace it.

Sheila Lawrence

It's interesting, because there's no swearing on network television, which is what I've mostly done, although it seems that every year we talked of a new word that was allowed. Like "hey guys, we've got *ass* now!" I always personally wondered why that was such an accomplishment – I wasn't particularly missing it. It's been weird now that I've been working on cable and some streaming shows and you can say everything, but I still jump a little bit when I see the word *fuck* in a script, like "whoa!" But I think there's two sides to it. On the one hand, I think people go to swear words way too easily, particularly in comedy because you add the word *fucking* in and make something edgier and funnier and it pops and it's shocking and it's an easy way to get a reaction. On the other hand, it sounds very, very fake to me [to use euphemisms]. Say you're writing a scene at a police station and the cops are saying "no friggin' way" and it kind of takes you out of the moment. If I were writing again on a show where you couldn't swear, I would probably tend to go around swear words, because no one says *friggin'*. So I'd just find another way of saying "I'm pissed off". But it's really, really hard, because there are some situations where swearing is what happens and anything else feels not true to the reality.

In life and in writing dialogue, a huge function of swear words is to just put a whole bunch of emotion into one sort of mini little explosion. And thus it tends to ring false if you try instead of the swear word to say "I am feeling so frustrated with the state of the world right now". The saying is "oh fuck!"

Robert Berens

I think what's allowed for any given show in terms of swearing and the content of swearing becomes an incredibly defining part of a voice of a show. And the fact that I, as a writer, can't say *fuck* on this show [*Supernatural*], when virtually every scenario is an "oh fuck" situation and Dean is not the kind of guy who doesn't say *fuck*, means there's an artifice built into specifically Dean's inability to say *fuck*. But all of our characters are people who would use the f-word and would use it freely. But as much as it's frustrating when I'm in a script room – like, there is no way he's not saying *fuck* here – this is where I think you get a lot of that, you know the *Buffy* slang or even a *Supernatural* in-show slang. A lot of that is an accommodation to not being able to curse. And so you come up with cute, acceptable alternatives. Even just watching the show, you know, you watch a season of the show and you know what you can get away with and what you can't.

But it's interesting because I think a lot of the voice of the show is actually that elision. Because as intense as our show gets, cursing can be ugly and it can be mean. And I think that the absence of cursing actually keeps a few sour notes out of the language of our show in a way that is defining and is probably for the better of the show. There's a whole other conversation that I won't get into, around the weird inconsistencies or paradoxes in terms of what's allowed and what's not, and so on certain shows and certain networks you can say *bitch* but you can't say *asshole*. Well that would be an example of a gendered double standard in terms of language.

Jane Espenson

It's great when you're allowed to do it [swearing], because you can have characters speak the way they'd speak. But on *Battlestar Galactica* where the swearing had been invented, that felt the same. If I could have a character say *frak*, it felt just as liberating because in their culture we knew what weight it carried. Well, maybe not *quite* as liberating, because we know it's not going to hit the audience with that visceral frisson of a real swear word.

I love when I'm at a cable show and I can "do swears". I love the swearing, but I am fine without it, because any time you put a limitation on a writer, it forces you to be more creative. Anyone who is never told "no", is not going to be interesting. Tell a writer "no" and make them get around the obstacle and they're going to come up with innovative solutions. *Frak* is an innovative solution. There's an old American show called *Kojak*, who was a character that would clearly be a smoker in "real" life – they gave him a lollipop and said he was quitting smoking. When you see that lollipop, it now has the same impact as a cigarette, without a cigarette. So smart. That's what *frak* does. I've gotten very few chances to use swearing in dialogue other than *frak*. But when you do, it's great because it's closer to real.

It probably feels a bit artificial to have characters who would clearly be swearing not swear. *NYPD Blue* is a situation where a cop would swear. So how does *NYPD Blue* handle it? They use words like *joint* to mean "dick". Where a real cop would say *dick*, they'd say *joint*. You want the viewer to be like "oh, I've never heard that slang". To say, like, "I'm not from New York, but I'm willing to believe that a New York cop would use that word". In fact, it starts to sound dirty to me; it's clear what it means – very much like *frak*, but without the need for a science fiction lexicon. So I always thought that was so smart. You hear the way he says that word, you know it's dirty, you get some of the effect of the swearing but you do it on network.

But other than that, when you have a grizzled detective saying "forget you!", it doesn't feel real. And there's only a certain amount that you can stretch the language to try to sound as good as a swear word. But you do what you can and you find smart ways to suggest that a swear word was *just about to* happen – cutting a character off, or an explosion happens. There was one show, *The Bonnie Hunt Show* I believe it was, that had the actor swear and bleeped it.

Summary and advice

There seems to be a consensus among the interviewed writers that swearing adds to realism, and, conversely, that not being allowed to use particular words creates artifice. At the same time, such restrictions represent a stimulus to writers to be creative and smart in their writing, because go-to euphemisms like *frigging* don't often work. Other functions of swearing are also identified, for example their use in characterization, expressing emotion, or creating a response in the audience. A general piece of advice we can take from this is the following: be aware of the relevant restrictions that apply and think about ways of creating realism without swearing where necessary. What alternative ways are there to fulfill the function that the swear word was meant to fulfill? What works for this character and the world they inhabit?

Note

1 The use of swear or taboo words is not gratuitous, but fulfills various functions within the televisual narrative, often multiple functions at the same time. These functions are illustrated in Monika Bednarek, "The multifunctionality of swear/taboo words in television series," in *Emotion in Discourse*, eds. J. Lachlan Mackenzie and Laura Alba-Juez (Amsterdam/Philadelphia: John Benjamins, 2019), pp. 31–57.

Reference

Bednarek, Monika. "The multifunctionality of swear/taboo words in television series." In *Emotion in Discourse*, edited by J. Lachlan Mackenzie and L. Alba-Juez. Amsterdam/Philadelphia: John Benjamins, 2019, pp. 31–57.

8 On dialect

Introductory remarks

Dialects are varieties of language that are associated with speakers from a geographical area (regional dialect) or social group (social dialect). The way regional or social dialects are portrayed in the media is often criticized by members of the public, by critics, or by scholars. This is therefore an area that screenwriters need to be aware of. In asking the five interviewees about dialect, I first explained that I was interested in dialects to do with region or ethnicity, and most often I provided relevant examples such as Southern characters or African American characters. I then asked a variant of the following question: "how do you go about representing, writing dialect?" I also posed the question: "what type of character would use" *ain't* and *y'all*, sometimes also asking "when would a character use" these words.

David Mandel

Obviously, done poorly it can be very embarrassing: every Southerner is not Foghorn Leghorn from the old Warner Brothers cartoons. Every guy from the South is not walking around going "I say, I say, I say, I say". Obviously, that's not what you want. And again in some cases, it's incredibly important, but often falls upon the actor. So for example, Sally Phillips is an actress who comes into the *Veep* world to play the character of Minna Häkkinen, and the character's Finnish, her nickname is "the Finnish wolf". The actor's somebody that just does immaculate research, and so she comes in prepared with a full, really quite perfect Finnish English-speaking accent. And so often she will take our sentences and the way she pronounces certain words, the way she'll change some sentence structure, and then obviously within her own adlibbing, of course makes us as writers look great. But it's incredibly important that there is that reality of sort of Finnish speaking.

This year we did a story in the South, in Alabama, and Tony Hale plays Gary, who's from Alabama, and while we didn't cast two other Alabama people, we cast two actors to be with him as his parents who were Southerners unto themselves, because we were trying to avoid these stereotypes.

Curb Your Enthusiasm has a very different model, because we don't have full scripts, we work from outlines that have lines of dialogue in them, but they're very much outlines. J.B. Smoove plays Leon Black – he moved in a couple of years ago and has never left. He's an African American male from New York. The last thing I want to do is tell him to say a line and add words like "hey homies" or anything else that further identifies me as an out-of-touch white guy. So often when we're talking about lines, we're talking very much about the idea, or we're saying here's the line we want, this is the information we want, and here's a line but we're not married to it, make it your own. And a couple of seasons back, he added "this is how we dos it". If I had written that, I don't think I would've ever written it. But all of a sudden he says "this is how we dos it", and he's pulling this from his own life experiences, but we're able to capture that on our show and therefore it's all the more authentic. And so it's incredibly important, and it's something the audience is particularly sensitive to now, because once upon a time seeing anyone that wasn't just white on television was somewhat of a rarity and that audience was ignored, and now there's an awareness of "oh wait, yes, other people do watch television other than white people". And so not only are they watching but they're going to judge and rightfully they should. Again you're striving for authenticity, and we'll do whatever we can to get it.

Further, we don't have a Finnish person in our writers' room, but obviously one hopes for diversity, and that's why there shouldn't just be a giant writers' room of twelve white guys, of the same background. We can talk about it ethnically, but we can also talk about different sexual orientations and also sex identities. It's not just language, specifics of language but also the process behind the language. These things will all fit together.

Doris Egan

You know, it depends. If it's a question where the dialect is really mostly coming out in accent as opposed to too much word change, then I certainly wouldn't write it. I assume the actor knows what they're doing and often you would get an actor from a particular place and if you can't, then they would work with a coach who can get them to the right place, and I would trust and hope that they would do that. It depends on how far the dialect is going. I had to do a Scotsman for *Reign*, and you're also affected by the fact that whatever it is he says has to be intelligible to a modern audience, a modern American audience, and you also don't want to sound like an idiot when you're writing, because how many Scotsmen from the 1500s have I hung with? Not that many. So I don't want to make too many missteps. But at the same time, there may be one or two words that you'll throw in. Like there's a moment where this guy is talking with Mary Queen of Scots who is a teenager in this version, and she is presenting herself to him as "your queen" and he's not really accepting it. She sends the message she'd like to speak with him privately – but she grew up in French court, and to his mind this is a girl who knows nothing of what we've been going through in Scotland, and she's sort of presuming with her "I am your queen and I want to speak to you". And so the first words out of his mouth are a casual, "well, lass, why am I here?" And his *lass* is not how you would address a queen. So I felt free to put that in, because it was saying something about his character and where he was at that moment, and they found an Edinburgh actor who needed to be told very little about how to do any of these things, so I was on board with that.

I was on a show once where we were all asked to do a lot of African American dialogue, semi-futuristic, but mostly not. And I was a little uncomfortable about it, because I felt that I didn't know enough – I hadn't been steeped in that as a cultural thing. And I just didn't want to make mistakes, basically, is what it comes down to. I did manage to do one episode that everyone seemed to like and I also worked closely with the actor. The character was Jamaican and the actor had spent time in Jamaica and knew a lot. So we worked it all out and I actually put dialogue in the script about the way he pronounces something. His wife was seeing an old boyfriend called Winston, which is a name you can come across in Jamaica, and so the character would say in this voice of doom, "*Ween*-ston". And I put that like W-E-E-N-ston, and everyone thought it was funny and it worked out. But on the whole, I leave that to the actor to a great extent.

Sheila Lawrence

I don't have a ton of experience writing dialects, but I always fear I'm writing a parody of the dialect. For example, the show I'm writing on now [*The Marvelous Mrs. Maisel*] is based around a New York Jewish family in the 50s. And there have been times where I'm writing something and it kind of sounds right but kind of sounds like a stereotype. So it's a tricky thing because these characters do not speak the way I speak, so you have to reflect that in the writing. But obviously, you want to be sensitive to doing it justice and not making it in any way cartoonish or stereotypical. I would say you try to capture it somewhat on the page, though it's a case of actors bringing something to it as well. You suggest it sometimes and then it just kind of becomes part of their performance, too.

Robert Berens

I think so much of that is dependent on the nature of the production, the nature of the show, and the nature of the cast. I would say if I'm writing a character from a specific background that's not this kind of generic white background, I would avoid being too voice-y or taking a swing at dialect, too specific in the hopes that that flavor, whatever that is, will come out from the actor that is cast in the role. I think that that generally is going to be a more authentic way to get that voice across than putting it on the page. That said, the script is also a tool for production – it's to be read, before it's to be filmed; it's to be read and it's to be understood. So adding a little bit of dialect flavor as a way of just communicating "this is the feeling of the character" as a shorthand can be necessary and be useful along the way. So ultimately, I would generally defer to the actor to bring that. But sometimes someone is playing something outside of their actual background, so you do want to work that flavor in. I've never had consultants for dialect, because I would say sometimes the actor brings it, sometimes you're just fudging it, you're just taking a swing at it on the page. The expectation and the hope is that the director and the actor will tailor it to make it as authentic or at least not as conspicuously inaccurate when you get to the set.

Jane Espenson

I worked on a show which used what's now called African American Vernacular English. I worked on a show with a black cast called *Me and the Boys* starring Steve Harvey who is brilliant, brilliant, brilliant, brilliant. We had a couple of his friends in the room who were African American comedians who knew him very well and knew how to capture how he spoke. But because the rest of us did not speak that dialect of English, the decision was made to just write it how we'd say it and Steve would translate it into his dialect of English. That worked very well. We weren't doing the sort of insulting thing of going like "this is how we think Black English works" which never goes well, and he was able to take the lines we'd written and make them sound natural to how he spoke.

And with British characters, they're going to say a), British stuff that Americans wouldn't say, b) stuff Americans *think* British people would say. There was stuff that I learned on *Torchwood* that I'd always had British characters say, and then I was working for an actual Brit who's going "no we don't actually say that". There is also a definite compulsion among American writers to make every British character sound very posh, and to use British terms all the time in their speech. Joss [Whedon] once said "Giles [in *Buffy*] is going to be British no matter how you write. The audience can hear him!"

And that was a big eye opener of: oh right, I don't need to indicate that Giles is British. This isn't a novel. Let the actor's accent do the work for you.

Not all scriptwriters are aware of the danger of stereotyping dialects. There is a thing that happens in casting: you're casting an intercity bus driver, and who gets sent to that audition? You're going to get sent 20 overweight African American ladies, because if I put that woman behind the wheel of the bus everyone's going to go "oh right she's the bus driver". You put a 75-year-old white lady with a fancy hairdo in that seat everyone's going to go like "oh, I guess she's the bus driver" and they're suddenly looking at that and not the rest of the scene. So it's always easier to cast to the stereotype. You have to make an effort not to do it. It's an effort that's worth doing, because you're just reinforcing everybody's stereotypes by casting for the stereotype. And I think language can do a similar thing where you're just like "oh I'll give them exactly what they expect this guy to talk like". The thing I enjoy doing is trying to cast against the type and write the dialogue against what you expect.

On the use of *ain't*

David Mandel

These days not a lot of characters [would use *ain't*]. People might use it ironically. I think they might use it to make fun of something that they think is stupid, or to try and make a point. But it might be more sarcastically, the incorrectness might help you make your point sarcastically. Again you might use it to make fun of somebody, like that person's dumb so you might do your impression of them and then add *ain't* in perhaps a way it wouldn't be used. I do think you might actually find a dumb character, who uses it because they don't know any better. Again those are very specific uses.

Doris Egan

I can think of three times to use *ain't*. One is obviously an uneducated character. The other is sometimes when a character's making a point like "this ain't rocket science!" And the third one is, there was a slang use of *ain't* among the British aristocracy in the 20s and 30s. It's fun to hear Lord Peter Wimsey or someone use the word *ain't*. And they could get away with it.

Robert Berens

I don't know how to unpack that just intuitively. And I would say that that would be a case where the racial politics of the use of that word would probably trip me up. Where I would feel comfortable, if I was conveying a kind of blue-collar, white terseness, I don't feel comfortable using an *ain't* if I was writing a black character. Throwing in an *ain't* would probably raise an issue and I think it speaks to what show you're writing for. Because ultimately you want to be authentic, ultimately you don't want to be offensive or limiting and it just depends, it's case-by-case.

Jane Espenson

Ain't is not in my idiolect, but I would use it in two situations that I can think of. One is if it would be in a character's dialect. Grumpy on *Once Upon a Time* speaks the *ain't* dialect. So if he were saying "she ain't there", I'd write *ain't*, because that's what I would hear in my head when I'm listening to the character. The other place I'd use it is the way *I'd* use it, which is a character quoting or trying to sound folksy or commenting on folksiness. So there's a common expression "hit 'em where they ain't", which means approach the situation from the approach no one else is taking. Then I can say it, and it sounds fine.

On the use of *y'all*

David Mandel

It's sort of a Southern thing in the sense of people *do* do it, but I'm not sure they're conscious of doing it. So it's almost a little insulting in a way to just write it in, so I would write in "are you coming?" or something like that, and leave it to the actor if that's how they naturally change their *you*s to *y'all*s. If I'm going to use it, and this is very much a comedy definition, I will probably use it if a character is making fun of themselves. I might have them hit the *y'all* for comedy reasons. It's just purposefully to break the ear a little bit, to hit it in a way, from a character you wouldn't expect to say it, because they're trying to make a point or be funny. So again it's a very specific thing.

Doris Egan

That's only Southern. I'm not sure I have written that. I have written some characters from the South, but they were usually in a formal setting, and *y'all* is both Southern and casual. Looking back I think I may have actually used it once or twice in my personal life, but it's really much more *you guys*.

Sheila Lawrence

Well, *that* I have written in a Southern show. So, I only think of that as a Southern thing. Either Southern characters or a character who's hanging out with some Southern people, who's just trying to be playful and sound like them – like "hey y'all come on in now". But it would mostly be a Southern character. From what I hear that is a thing people actually say, so it is not mocking Southern culture.

Robert Berens

I don't think I've ever put *y'all* in a script. But maybe that's because I just don't write enough Southern characters.

Jane Espenson

That is rarer than *ain't. Y'all* is very Southern, but it is very useful, because we don't have a second person plural. So I have even used it myself when I am finding myself really pressed to make the distinction between *you* and *y'all*. And I grew up saying *all of you* or *you guys* for that, and in the Midwest *all of you* serves the same function as *y'all*. But at a certain point I forgot *all of you* and started using a self-conscious *y'all*, not a very natural one. I don't know that I've ever written that in dialogue though.

I think sometimes *y'all* is an easy way to say "this character's Southern", instead of genuinely thinking about how they would really talk. Even though I have on occasion used it, it would not be a thing it would occur to me to write for a character, though now I'm looking forward to an opportunity to use it, because there's something whimsical about it. Southern characters just haven't been on my shows. But there's something funny about a non-Southerner using it, just because they find themselves backed into a corner where they linguistically need it.

Summary and advice

The interviewed writers make it clear that they are aware of the dangers of stereotyping and errors in writing dialect. They would therefore avoid being too specific in their writing, but might add some dialect flavor in the script to indicate a character's identity to casting. Often, it seems to be left up to the actors to provide the necessary authenticity through their own dialect or accent.

In terms of advice, it is crucial to be aware of the fact that stereotypes and bias are not just created by casting to the stereotype or by endowing particular kinds of characters with particular kinds of personality traits. Stereotypes can also be created by how characters use language. An example of a linguistic stereotype would be if a TV series includes a range of characters that are all *equally* likely to use a stigmatized form such as *ain't*, but the only character to use the word is an African American character. Avoid creating stereotypes in the way characters use language, unless it is your express intention to do so, for example for dramatic or humorous purposes (if appropriate). Do some research about how people use language or ask for advice from someone who knows, or hold back and leave it largely up to the actors. This applies especially but not just to "minority" characters.

9 Conclusion

In this book I have presented edited and curated extracts from my interviews with five television writers and have provided brief summaries and general advice at the end of each chapter. As mentioned in the introduction, this advice is based on the interviews, occasionally supplemented by insights from my own research. Five points are important to keep in mind:

First, the advice focuses on the *dialogue* section of scripts rather than other elements such as action lines or parentheticals. In addition, the advice deliberately focuses on the specifics of language use. Other aspects of screenwriting are widely covered in "how to" manuals.

Second, what we hear on screen differs partially from dialogue in the script, because actors can make changes when performing the script (the extent to which this is allowed depends on the particular series) and dialogue can also be edited in the edit room.

Third, some aspects of dialogue are left up to the actors rather than being scripted by writers, but to find out who is responsible for a particular word or effect in a dialogue line we would need access to the whole production process. Importantly, it is *not* the case that words and expressions such as *well* (to start a sentence), *you know, like*, and *I mean* (as discourse markers), *um* and *uh* (for hesitation), *ain't*, *y'all*, or the emphasis on words (*I'm so sorry*) are exclusively introduced by actors in their performance. My search of 17 official final scripts archived in the Writers Guild Foundation's Shavelson-Webb Library in Los Angeles found that all of these expressions occur in some of the investigated scripts. Some TV scripts also use underlining or italics to identify that a word should be emphasized or employ dot points or other devices to mark pauses, hesitation, or the like within a speaker's utterance.

Fourth, when we think about writing dialogue or how characters would talk, we always need to relate this to the particular context of a series, for example whether it is broadcast or cable or streaming, the genre, the setting, the nature of the characters, the world that they inhabit, and so on.

Finally, writing for a TV series is a collaborative endeavor and it is important to understand the process whereby a script comes into being – for example, whether a writers' room is used and how the writers' room works for a particular series. In the US, the structure, plots, and scenes for an episode are typically developed collaboratively. Script drafts produced by a writer will need to be modified by the writer based on various types of feedback or may be rewritten by others. It is useful to consult more detailed explanations of this process, which are available in many screenwriting manuals (see also the chapter on the writers' room in *Writing Hollywood*, by Patricia Phalen, Routledge, 2018).

While I have identified some key points arising from the interview answers in the brief summaries and relevant advice at the end of each chapter, my intention in this book was to let the material speak for itself rather than to speak to the material. Hearing directly from screenwriting professionals about aspects to do with language can complement other available resources that have different purposes. I hope that presenting the material in this way is useful to anyone interested in the craft of screenwriting and the creation of constructed language.

Reference

Phalen, Patricia F. *Writing Hollywood: The Work and Professional Culture of Television Writers*. London/New York: Routledge, 2018.

Index

For Product Safety Concerns and Information please contact our EU representative GPSR@taylorandfrancis.com
Taylor & Francis Verlag GmbH, Kaufingerstraße 24, 80331 München, Germany

www.ingramcontent.com/pod-product-compliance
Lightning Source LLC
LaVergne TN
LVHW010942110826
845149LV00013B/2729

* 9 7 8 1 0 3 2 1 7 8 4 0 0 *